Featured on ABC TV's *Good Morning America!*, National Public Radio, and radio stations around the country.

Recommended by the *New York Times Syndicate, Travel Weekly, Woman's Day, Bottom Line Tomorrow, New Choices, RV Times Magazine, Foremost Living Trends, Adventure Road, Washington Flyer.*

"For the person who's been everywhere but couldn't or didn't take the time to stop and smell the flowers, this books details thousands of ways to travel and learn. A cornucopia of ideas for travelers."
Way to Go column, *The New York Times Syndicate.*

"Kaye has penned an easy-to-read, easy-to-use guide that will help those planning an educational vacation."   *Birmingham News.*

"*Travel and Learn* is a valuable source book with unusual programs for travelers who want to learn more about the country they're visiting and meet local experts who lead them off the beaten track."
Bon Voyage Column.

"A handy and concise reference guide to educational vacation programs sponsored by organizations and colleges across the U.S. Kaye has assembled useful information about a wide variety of hands-on programs both here and abroad. Clearly written and well-organized. This book makes for good browsing for travelers willing to go the extra mile and educate themselves about what's available."
American Library Association Booklist.

"For an inveterate traveler and an always-learner, this book is perfect."
Lewiston Tribune.

"The guide to vacations that are good for you! The hottest news in travel today is the education vacation. The range of choices is amazing." *Mature Choices.*

"The learning isn't just schooling either; it's exploring the horse-based cultures of Central Mongolia, taking in the lesser ruins of Mexico and Central America with archaeologists, or staying in America to meet Indians face to face." *Hickory News.*

"*Travel and Learn* is the perfect resource for people who prefer their vacations to provide a learning experience." *The Rotarian.*

"If you're an active traveler who likes to learn while experiencing new and exciting locations, then *Travel and Learn* is for you." *Family Magazine.*

"Refreshing entry into the crowded travel field. Many travelers should find *Travel and Learn* a useful sourcebook and wonderful idea book." *Morgan Directory Reviews.*

"Among the most interesting and unique guides I've seen this year." *Greenwich Time.*

"The range of destinations and diversions should excite even the most sophisticated traveler or scholar." *Grand Times.*

Awards:

National Mature Media Award/Travel Books
Midwest Independent Publishers Association
Best Travel Books 1994, Gourmet Magazine

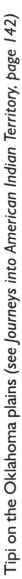

Robert Vetter

Tipi on the Oklahoma plains (see *Journeys into American Indian Territory*, page 142)

TRAVEL AND LEARN

1001 Vacations

Around the World

Fourth Edition

Evelyn Kaye

BLUE PANDA PUBLICATIONS
BOULDER, COLORADO

Travel and Learn, Fourth Edition by Evelyn Kaye

Published by Blue Panda Publications
3031 Fifth Street
Boulder, Colorado 80304
Email: ekaye@amexol.net
Web: www.travelbooks123.com

Book design: Christopher Sarson
Cover: George Roche Design

Every effort has been made to make certain of the accuracy of the information in this book, but the world of travel changes from day to day. The publisher takes no responsibility for inaccuracies relating to the material included. Readers are urged to contact the organizations directly before making travel plans.

© Copyright 2001 by Evelyn Kaye
Fourth Edition
Printed in the United States of America

ISBN 1-929315-01-5
Library of Congress Catalog Number 2001129025

THE AUTHOR

Evelyn Kaye's travels began when she sailed to Canada from England as a child with her grandmother and ended up living in Toronto for almost four years. She's traveled ever since. After school in England, she lived for a year in France, and in Israel. She's toured Italy, Sicily, Denmark, Sweden, Belgium, the Netherlands, Switzerland, Mexico, Ecuador, Australia, New Zealand, and India. She's sailed round the Galapagos Islands, camped in the Amazon rainforest, rafted through the Grand Canyon, horse-packed along the beaches of Venezuela, walked across volcanoes in Hawaii, and hiked in the Rocky Mountains. She's also visited Antarctica to marvel at penguins and icebergs, patted whales in Baja California, and followed Isabella Bird's footsteps through northern Japan.

As a writer and journalist in England, she was the first woman reporter in the *Manchester Guardian*'s newsroom, and was a reporter with Reuters News Agency in Paris. In the United States, her articles have been published in the *New York Times, Denver Post, McCalls, New Choices, New York* magazine, *Travel & Leisure*, and other major publications. She is founder of Colorado Independent Publishers Association, past president of the American Society of Journalists and Authors, and is listed in *Who's Who in America*. She lives in Boulder, Colorado.

BOOKS BY EVELYN KAYE

Travel and Learn, (4th edition, Blue Panda, 2001; 3rd edition, Blue Penguin, 1995; 2nd edition, Blue Penguin, 1992; 1st edition, 1990, Blue Penguin)

Adventures in Japan (Blue Panda, 2000)

Amazing Traveler: Isabella Bird (2nd edition, Blue Panda, 1999; 1st edition, Blue Penguin, 1994)

Free Vacations & Bargain Adventures in the USA (2nd edition, Blue Panda, 1998; 1st edition, Blue Penguin, 1995)

Active Woman Vacation Guide (Blue Panda, 1997)

Family Travel (Blue Penguin, 1993)

Eco-Vacations (Blue Penguin, 1991) Quality Paperback Book Club selection

College Bound with J. Gardner (College Board, 1988)

The Parents Going-Away Planner with J. Gardner (Dell, 1987)

The Hole In The Sheet (Lyle Stuart, 1987)

Write and Sell Your TV Drama! with A. Loring (ALEK, 1984; revised, 1993)

Relationships in Marriage and the Family with Stinnett and Walters (Macmillan, 1984)

Crosscurrents: Children, Families & Religion (Clarkson Potter, 1980)

The Family Guide to Cape Cod with B. Chesler (Barre/Crown, 1979)

The ACT Guide to Childrens Television (Beacon Press, 1979)

The Family Guide to Childrens Television (Pantheon, 1975)

Action for Childrens Television, Editor (Avon, 1972)

"Too often travel, instead of broadening the mind, merely lengthens the conversation." Elizabeth Drew

CONTENTS

The old city, Strasbourg, France

"Travel is fatal to prejudice, bigotry and narrow-minded-
ness, all foes to real understanding. Likewise tolerance, or
broad, wholesome, charitable views of men and things
cannot be acquired by vegetating in our little corner of
the earth all one's lifetime."   Mark Twain

INTRODUCTION
TO THE FOURTH EDITION

The aim of this book is to offer you a selection of the
best educational travel choices that are available around the
world. I've interpreted education in its broadest sense to
include a wide range of learning experiences — academic,
physical, artistic, and practical. This new fourth edition of
Travel and Learn is completely revised and updated and has
much more information than before, including email and
web sites.

Today, educational travel has come into its own. The fast-
est growing segment of the travel and tourism field is the
adult education vacation. Travelers today are becoming more
and more sophisticated because the more you travel, the
more you want from a vacation. You look for value, interest, and stimulation, not just time to laze on the beach or
relax in a hammock.

There is an amazing assortment of opportunities. In this
book you'll find how to join archaeological digs in Colorado,
take a house building course in Massachusetts, follow history tours of Civil War sites, go river rafting on the Salmon
River in Idaho, study pottery with a Native American potter

and her family in California, or stay at a dude ranch and play cowboy on the trails. You can enjoy delicious cooking classes in France and Italy, live on a homestay with a family in Russia, join a walking tour of Japan and sleep in traditional inns, see tigers and giraffes on African safaris, paddle a sea kayak and watch whales, or sign up for dozens of language programs including German, French, Spanish, Italian, Greek, Hebrew, Japanese and Chinese.

Some organizations offer dozens of national and international programs, such as the Smithsonian Associates. Others specialize in particular areas; the American Horticultural Society offers tours to beautiful gardens, and Spirit of India specializes in travels in India. It is the quality of the program that counts.

Why I wrote the book

I've taken many educational trips myself. My Itchy Feet Syndrome, a case of severe travelitis, makes me welcome any opportunity to travel, and over the years, I've learned to fit everything I need into a carry-on bag, use a travel-hardy camera, wear comfortable easy-care clothes, take good walking shoes, and practice my yoga breathing to cope with crises.

The more I traveled, the more I longed to find a book like this, a book that puts together trips that offer more than just a visit but take you to see places in depth. I enjoy discovering the stories about the places I see. I want to know more about the countries I tour. I want to meet experts who can take me to interesting sights off the beaten track. I love learning words and phrases in a new language.

But I could never find the right book. So I decided I would have to write it myself.

This new kind of travel book is designed to meet the needs of a new breed of traveler. It's for those who want to learn as they roam and like to expand their horizons and find new challenges. It's for the woman who takes off for a bicycle tour of Africa though she hasn't pedaled a bike since high school, or for the man who signs up for a college course in Tibetan mythology because the topic fascinates him. It's for the active couple who decide to spend a vacation assisting a research project on sea turtles in California, or for the retired accountant who longs to dig for dinosaurs with paleontologists. It's for the Sunday painter who wants a week to capture the landscape, and the gourmet who's always wanted to learn the secrets of French cuisine. It's for the active hikers who long to walk through Italy staying at delightful inns and the rafting enthusiasts who dream of floating through the canyons of western America.

Selected companies

Every company in TRAVEL AND LEARN has been carefully selected for the quality of their programs. The hundreds of vacations recommended in this book were chosen based on extensive research including questionnaires, the Internet, printed materials, and phone interviews. Every listing in the book complied with the TRAVEL AND LEARN criteria and each company must:

✓ offer quality educational programs;
✓ provide qualified leaders for trips and programs;
✓ have been in business for a reasonable period of time;
✓ have run successful trips before;
✓ provide helpful informational material;
✓ answer questions promptly;
✓ explain clearly what prices include;
✓ welcome inquiries;
✓ list an address and phone in the US;
✓ provide names and addresses of recent participants.

Universities, colleges, museums and educational groups offer educational travel to students, alumni, and associates. Most trips are open to all though non-students may have to pay a fee to become a member or an associate. There may be reading lists and you can sometimes earn academic credits. Some institutions use professional travel agencies that specialize in educational tours led by experts who give seminars and lectures along the way. Some trips take you to places the average traveler doesn't see; a trip to Nepal includes informal visits to homes, or a visit to a shaman healer in an Ecuadorian rainforest.

New Style Travel

Some travel guide books look down on groups. There's a distinct feeling that it's a sign of weakness to travel with a group. True Travelers must wander about alone, peer at the major sights which they find unaided, struggle to choose a room, a meal, a bath, and never admit they don't know what's going on. You are supposed to be strong enough to do it on your own or it doesn't count.

For those of us who travel frequently on airplanes, trains, buses, cars or tours, we've learned that the hassles of traffic, the impersonal crowds at airports, the delays on trains and roads are the same around the world. You spend too much time doing things you hoped to avoid. Too many airports look alike, too many hotels have American names, and too many restaurants offer fast-food service. What's more, it's never been much fun trying to find a room at midnight in a strange city with no place to cash a check and where no one speaks your language.

If you really want to avoid the tourists, meet the local people, and travel off the beaten path, you are better off going with a local guide or someone who knows the area and can take you behind the scenes. My most interesting trips have happened not when I'm alone but when I'm with someone who knows the area I'm visiting.

And there's one unmentionable little travel secret that no travel writer ever likes to admit. Few travel writers ever travel alone. Most often they travel in groups, taken from place to place by local guides who want to make sure they have a wonderful time. Even experienced travel writers who set out alone know that the best way to be shown round a new place is to find a local guide who will help them in finding exactly what they want to see.

I have discovered that it can be most enriching to join travel programs sponsored by a university or museum or educational organization where the expertise and knowledge of a qualified leader expands your understanding and eliminates the hassles of everyday living so you can focus on the fascinating.

Learning Travel is Booming

Today, for many reasons, there is a boom in learning vacations. Americans have always wanted to make the best use of their time, and the idea of learning something useful on vacation has a definite appeal. For many people, it's the opportunity to follow their dream and take a vacation that focuses on the topics that entrance, intrigue or fascinate them. But the boom also reflects changes in modern society.

Better Education: With more and more people completing high school and college, first-time travelers don't want a haphazard trip to an unknown place. It's more fun to study the language and culture of a country or to take a seminar on art and architecture, or to listen to a scientist explain how volcanoes develop. You gain more from travel with experts.

Aging Population: A growing percentage of our population is over 40, so that older Americans outnumber younger

Americans. But since American men and women between 40 and 70 enjoy better health, more energy, more money, and more leisure time than their parents ever did, they have an enthusiasm for travel but no longer want the hassles of bookings and tickets and arrangements. They may be widowed or divorced, or have a spouse who hates to leave home, so they choose the companionship of a tour and travel with others who share their interests.

More Trips, More Choices: A few years ago, only a handful of organizations offered learning vacations. Today the list keeps growing — from colleges that run seminars to the craft museum that tours potters' studios to the wilderness organization that leads trips to nature preserves .

In this book you'll discover a wide selection of the best learning travel programs available and a range of opportunities for your next vacation based on the most up-to-date research available.

A journey is always unique and quite unpredictable, like falling in love. We travel with our individual views, expectations, and attitudes. We may travel to the same places but at different times and with new companions and under circumstances that can never be replicated. The weather always changes, a view of famous sights becomes a sudden glimpse of wonder, the group of traveling strangers melds into a band of laughing friends. Every trip promises a special adventure, and the pleasant thrill of surprise.

I'd be delighted to hear from any traveler who takes a learning vacation. Just drop me a note and recommend what you find, and I'll include it in the next edition.

Here's hoping you have wonderful journeys, and may all your dreams come true.

Happy traveling!

Evelyn Kaye

"If God had really intended men to fly, He'd have made it easier to get to the airport."   Anon.

HOW TO USE THIS BOOK

This book is a Travel Resource Guide. It's a guide to use when you are thinking about vacations, an idea book to suggest places, activities and vacation experiences you may never have thought about and to outline what they are like, what you can expect, where you can find them, and how much they cost. Think of it as a learning travel map for you to discover where you'd like to go.

The book has three sections. The first describes different topics for learning vacations and a short list of the companies offering those vacations. The second section is an alphabetical listing of companies with complete details of how to contact them, what they offer, and comments from people who have taken their trips. The third section is a useful collection of travel resources.

SECTION I

Here's where you find out about seven categories of learning vacations: Adventure Outdoors, Archaeology and History, Arts, Crafts, Language and Culture, Nature and Wildlife, and Waterways.

SECTION 2

From A to Y (couldn't find a Z company name!) provides an alphabetical listing of the companies offering learning vacations with complete details of how to contact them, descriptions of their programs, comments from participants, prices of popular trips and what's included. Prices generally cover:

Accommodations: Luxury or comfortable hotel, university dorm, college room, houseboat, cruise ship, apartment, villa, cabin, hut, tent, or sleeping pad — always ask before you go. Sometimes the cost of accommodations for the day before or after a trip is not included in the overall price, and you may need to budget for one or two nights in a hotel. If you like a firm mattress or cannot sleep with street noise or have special needs, make sure you make that clear in advance.

Escorts, Guides, Leaders, Lecturers: Many trips have an escort or leader, who organizes the tickets, bookings and everyday necessities, and a guide or lecturer, who is an expert in the area or the subject. Find out who will be traveling with you, what their qualifications are, and how long they have been leading groups. Most organizations carefully choose leaders and guides for their experience, knowledge, and abilities, and are happy to give you the information.

Meals: Take note of how many meals are provided. "Some Meals" usually include breakfast and a few lunches or dinners, but the rest of the time you buy your own. "Most Meals" means that you will only have to buy an occasional lunch or dinner and everything else is included. "All Meals" means just what it says. Most organizations provide special diets or vegetarian menus if you request them in advance. Often some of the best meals are served on outdoor adventure and nature trips where creative cooks whip up gourmet cuisine on a camp stove.

Transportation: This covers travel once you've reached your starting destination. Taking a bus, train, plane, and boat during the program is included under transportation. It's a good idea to ask how much additional travel there will be, what extra costs may total, and details of what's involved. Besides, it's nice to know there'll be an elephant ride in the jungle or a carriage ride through the historic section of an old city.

Permits, Entry Fees: These cover entrance fees to museums, parks, castles, and sites of interest. You can ask for an estimate of the total cost of these items before you leave. Also ask if you should budget any money for tips.

Tours, Excursions: These are trips to places of interest lasting a day, a weekend, or longer. Before you sign up, you can ask the organization which places you will be visiting. If there are sights you are particularly interested in seeing, you can make sure there will be an opportunity to do so.

Airfare: Only a few companies include international or other airfares in their prices. Many can arrange for a group travel fare for you if you'd like them to book it. Others can let you travel on you own and meet the group at an assigned place. Make sure you check what travel costs are included.

SECTION 3

Here you'll find helpful travel web sites, a short book list, and names and addresses of state and foreign tourist offices so you can contact them directly for more information.

And finally a word of travel advice.

GO WITH THE FLOW

Every care has been taken to make sure that the information, trip details and prices described are accurate as the book goes to press. But travel is like a river, always changing. All information and prices are subject to unexpected variations, so please recognize that the costs quoted are only guidelines and cannot be guaranteed.

Evelyn Kaye

Hakodate Fish Market, Japan

"That woman speaks eighteen languages, and can't say
No in any of them."   Dorothy Parker

SECTION 1: TOPICS

You've decided to take an educational travel vacation. Sounds great — but what would you like to learn about? What kind of educational experience are you looking for? How will you make the right choice among the hundreds of programs available today to those who want to travel and learn?

My interpretation of education is in its widest and most far-reaching sense. For those of us who remember school, we know that some learning takes place in classrooms. If you've ever been lucky enough to study with a teacher who loves her subject, you know that the best education takes place when an eager student meets an enthusiastic teacher whose knowledge and interest brings everything about the topic alive.

I once joined a nature walk in upstate New York to look for mushrooms, an aspect of nature about which I know exceptionally little. Our leader was an easy-going articulate professor who was passionate about mushrooms and a re-nowned international expert. He spotted a variety of large and small fungi that our eyes were too ignorant to see, explained why they grow where they do and how you can find them, told us fascinating stories of mushrooms he'd met along the way, and those he still wanted to find. I still remember the exhilaration of listening to his voice as he pointed to a pure white death angel, a highly poisonous mushroom standing alone under a shadowy tree, looking so tempting and yet so innocent. His knowledge and enthusiasm made that walk a peak learning experience for me.

An educational vacation includes the academic, intellectual, artistic, and the physical. You can choose an active physical adventure and try hiking, rowing, paddling, climbing, swimming, fishing, bicycling or horse-riding. Or you can choose a more intellectual journey and study painting, sculpture, design, or theater, or practice the crafts of pottery, weaving, batik, or silkscreen, or join programs in music and dance, writing and literature.

The Topics are broad areas of study to give you an idea about where you'd like to go and what you'd like to do. There are seven major areas:

Adventure Outdoors, includes walking, hiking, climbing, biking.

Archaeology and History, explores different aspects of the past.

Arts, includes painting, sculpture, literature, theater, music, photography.

Crafts, includes pottery, weaving, traditional crafts, cooking.

Language and Culture, where you learn the language and experience the culture.

Nature and Wildlife, to study flora, fauna, birds, animals, dinosaurs.

Waterways, includes travel on rivers, oceans, lakes.

After each topic section, there is a list of the organizations offering trips.

You can follow your interests wherever they may lead. Explore the past and walk over Civil War battlefields, or look to the future with trips that examine research in environmental sciences and ecology. Visit Yellowstone to learn about nature and the wilderness, go on safari in Africa, or raft down hidden waterways in Australia. Choose from hundreds of language programs in dozens of countries where you can perfect your Spanish, Swedish, or Swahili. Live abroad and experience poetry, politics, and performances. Take classes in gourmet cooking, social issues, British detective novels, or American Indian dance.

Take a chance! Try something you've never studied before — or something you've always wanted to know more about. Now is always the best time to begin!

ADVENTURE OUTDOORS

"The backpack was heavy; my shoulders and hips hurt; trails were long and all gain; mosquitoes were abundant and hungry; when it wasn't raining it was hailing. So how do I feel about the Women's Beginner Backpack Trip? I loved it! I have come away from Yosemite feeling stronger and surer."

That's how a woman from California summed up her first experience of backpacking on a backpacking trip with a group of women who had never done it before. The joys of exploring beautiful scenery entice thousands of people out into the mountains and hills to hike, trek, and backpack through national and state parks, or to ski along peaceful trails through snowy landscapes in winter. Today, there are also some companies that specialize in adventure trips for women only.

Walking and hiking are the simplest ways to explore the great outdoors. You need a comfortable pair of walking shoes or lightweight boots, and you're on your way, walking through villages and towns, or following marked trails under the trees, carrying a pack on your back. On day hikes, you only need to take lunch, water, rain gear, and personal items. You may spend the night at a base camp in a tent, or in a lodge, cabin, or hotel. Longer hikes — often called treks — show you wonderful wilderness areas that you can reach only on foot and where you may be one of the few people to visit. A full backpack holds camping equipment, food, clothes, and personal needs. If you prefer, choose trips where llamas, donkeys, mules, or sturdy porters carry the gear, while you walk with a day pack.

Hiking can be done at any age, and several of the companies in the book welcome older hikers as well as young children. You will discover some of the most magnificent natural scenery in the world in dozens of state and national parks in the United States and abroad. In California, there are the wonders of Yosemite, in Montana and Wyoming you can explore Yellowstone with its astonishing hot springs, in Colorado you can see mountain sheep and elk in Rocky Mountain National Park, and on Cape Cod National Seashore you can stroll along untouched beaches and among windswept sand dunes.

Abroad, you can hike through the Alps in Europe and visit picturesque Swiss villages or French wine-growing towns. You can stroll along ramblers' paths in England and stay in thatched cottages or simple hostels. You can follow ancient Inca trails in Peru, Chile, and Ecuador, trek in the Andes to the hidden city of Machu Picchu, or follow the paths in the Himalaya to soaring snow-covered peaks.

Many established outdoor organizations specialize in hiking and are eager to help answer your questions. Most offer a range of trips for beginners, intermediates, and seasoned hikers. Some trips last for a weekend, a few days, or a week, while others last for several weeks or longer. You decide how much time you have, where you'd like to travel, and how energetic you feel, and then take off to discover the exhilaration of the natural world.

Bicycle trips offer a speedier view of the scenery. You may carry your gear on the bike as you pedal through the countryside on side roads and winding lanes, with stops at interesting towns and fascinating sights. Most bike trips are geared for different levels of expertise and provide a support van to carry the luggage, and pick up those whose heart is willing but legs can't make the hills. On some bike trips, you camp or stay in hostels; others offer hotels and gourmet meals along the way.

If you'd prefer a four-legged ride, try a horse-packing trip. Here, you follow tree-shaded trails, climb mountain paths, or canter along the beach on your travels. Some trips are based in rural lodges. On others you camp out along the way and horses or mules carry the equipment. You can find horsepacking trips around the world, offering English or Western style riding.

For the enthusiast who likes adventure, there are dozens of outdoor opportunities to learn climbing, mountaineering, skiing, and wilderness survival. For those who'd like to learn how to raft, canoe, kayak, and sail, check the section on Waterways.

Adventure Outdoor Organizations

Adventure Bound River Expeditions
AdventureWomen
Africa Travel Center
Alaska Wildland Adventures
Arctic Treks
Baja Discovery
Boojum Expeditions
Boulder Outdoor Survival School
Camp Denali & North Face Lodge
Canyonlands Field Institute
Ciclismo Classico
Country Inns Along the Trail
Cross Country Equestrian

Denali Backcountry Lodge
Denali Wilderness Lodge
Dude Ranchers Association
Echo: The Wilderness Company
Experience Plus!
Eldertreks
International Bicycle Fund
International Expeditions
James Henry River Journeys
Journeys International
Lindblad Expeditions
Maine Windjammers
Myths and Mountains

Adventure Outdoor Organizations (continued)

North Cascades Institute   The World Outdoors
Northern Lights Expeditions   UC Research Expeditions
Overseas Adventure Travel   Wilderness Travel
River Travel Center   Wildland Adventures
Rocky Mountain River Tours   Yellowstone Association Institute
Sea Quest Expeditions

ARCHAEOLOGY and HISTORY

Studying history is a way of understanding the past and its relationship to the present. There are a variety of travel programs that introduce travelers to ancient history and archaeology, and to more recent history in Europe, South America, and the United States. In traveling, you discover the reality of history in old buildings and monuments that are a living reminder of what happened before.

Many travel programs take time to point out the historical highlights as you travel so that as you bicycle through an Italian village, you stop to admire the old Roman bridges and the cobbled streets, As you hike along a path in the north of England, you see the remains of Hadrian's Wall which was erected by the Romans when they conquered the country.

In Colorado's Four Corners region there once was a thriving center with thousands of inhabitants in the 12th century, when, for some reason, they left their homes and abandoned the area. Today, you can spend a week as a volunteer and assist researcher archaeologists who are trying to discover why the Puebloan people left by digging up the remains of the stone buildings they erected and examining the tools, belongings and pottery scattered across the area.

Dinosaurs once roamed across the high plateaus of the American West. You can join programs to help paleontologists dig for dinosaurs in recognized sites where many bones have already been found.

Historical tours take you to Civil War sites, or to travel
through New Mexico to follow the footsteps of Billy the
Kid and his short and violent life. In West Virginia, you learn
the old folk arts of Appalachia through music, dancing,
storytelling, basket-making, and quilting.

Aboard an old-fashioned windjammer, you sail down the
Maine coast just the way sailors used to do, enjoying the
wind flapping the sails, and the leisurely pace of the vessel.
On a unique expedition to share the lives of today's American Indians, you sleep in a tipi and learn about the use of
medicinal plants, healing traditions, and spiritual principles.

You can walk round centuries old temples and houses in
Kyoto, Japan and see a way of life that still survives, or explore the traditional inns and pathways of the Japanese Alps.
In China, you can travel on the Yangtze River to see old
villages and landmarks that will disappear when the new dam
is completed.

In Peru, you can walk round the incredible city of Macchu
Picchu, set among the mountains and completely abandoned,
and in Mexico you can visit Mayan temples and statues dating back hundreds of years. In France, an artist helps you
study the famous paintings in the caves of Lascaux where
the 15,000-year-old drawings of horses, bison, and deer
were hidden for centuries. In Bhutan, you observe the sacred Tantric Dance Festival attended for centuries by pilgrims from around the country who honor their historic
celebration.

Archaelogy and History Organizations

Africa Travel Center
American Museum of Natural History
Arctic Treks
Art Trek
Augusta Heritage Center
British Studies at Oxford
Campbell Folk School
Canyonlands Field Institute
Centrum
Ciclismo Classico
Cross Cultural Journeys
Crow Canyon Archaeological Center

Archaelogy and History Organizations (continued)

Cuahnahuac
Danu Enterprises
Denver Museum of
    Nature and Science
Esprit Travel
Experience Plus!
HistoryAmerica Tours
Journeys Into
    American Indian Territory
Myths and Mountains
National Audubon Society
National Trust for Historic
    Preservation

Overseas Adventure Travel
Saga Holidays
Smithsonian Study Tours
Spirit of India
TraveLearn
Tuscan Way
University of California-Berkeley
UC Research Expeditions
University of New Orleans
University of Pennsylvania
University of Rhode Island
University of Wisconsin-Madison
Yellowstone Association Institute

ARTS

Your day job may fill your time but you still dream of becoming an artist and working creatively. On a learning vacation, you can experiment with what it would feel like to spend all your time painting, listening to music, writing, or simply studying beautiful art wherever you find it.

First ask yourself, are you a Viewer or a Do-er? Viewers like to look, observe, browse, think, and consider the arts. Do-ers like to do something active and sketch a landscape, play the ukelele, take photos, write a journal, practice square dancing.

For viewers, take guided tours led by arts experts to see some of the great paintings and sculptures of the world. Such tours are often offered by art museums in the area where you live. You can visit different museums and places of artistic interest, such as Provence in France to glimpse the views that inspired Impressionist painters or take a barge and float down the canals through scenery which inspired those glowing paintings of low bridges hung with ivy, picturesque villages, and yellow cornfields dotted with poppies.

Photography programs take you to Mexico or Africa or Australia, where experts teach you to take unforgettable pictures.

Music programs invite you to listen to concerts, see ballets in classic performance halls, or attend folk music, jazz, and blue-grass festivals. Experienced musicians can attend a bassoon camp or a chamber-music workshop to play in harmony with others. Other programs offer music and dancing. You can learn to tap dance, do Appalachian clog dances, or pick up American swing dances. One couple from New Jersey goes on an annual vacation to square dance workshops offered in different parts of the country.

Active artists can find dozens of programs around the country which offer summer courses in painting, sketching, landscape drawing, silkscreen, and more. There are also courses for those interested in literature and poetry; you can go hiking amid the soaring Cascades mountain range near Sedro Woolley, Washington as part of an outdoor seminar in poetry and prose readings about nature. Travel abroad to stay at Oxford University and study English literature, or venture into programs in Spanish, Russian, German, Italian, or an advanced program of French literature in Paris at the Sorbonne. Spend time in London attending theater performances with special visits backstage.

One educational trip takes participants to live at a British university with a trip to Shakespeare's home, Stratford-upon-Avon, and to attend seminars by eminent scholars on English literature, poetry, and drama.

Arts Organizations

Arrowmont School of Arts and Crafts
Art Trek
Ashokan Fiddle and Dance
Augusta Heritage Center
British Studies at Oxford
Campbell Folk School
Canyonlands Field Institute
Centro di Cultura Italiana in Casentino

Arts Organizations (continued)

Centrum
Ciclismo Classico
Cross Cultural Journeys
Crow Canyon Archaeological Center
Cuahnahuac
Danu Enterprises
Dillman's Creative Art Workshops
Esprit Travel
Experience Plus!
Friends of Fiber Art International
Glickman-Popkin Bassoon Camp
Idyllwild Arts
Journeys East
National Registration Center
    for Study Abroad

National Trust for Historic
    Preservation
Saga Holidays
Smithsonian Study Tours
Spirit of India
TraveLearn
Tuscan Way
University of California-Berkeley
University of New Orleans
University of Pennsylvania
University of Rhode Island
University of Wisconsin-Madison
Wildland Adventures

CRAFTS

Traveling to different parts of the world to see the wide variety of crafts can prove an enriching and exciting experience. You can live in an Italian villa and learn the secrets of Tuscany's peasant cuisine or spend time in a chateau in France and practice the joys of elegant French cooking. Food is a fascinating part of travel, and learning to cook in a different country is a unique introduction to a different culture.

Pottery and clay is another international craft. You can watch traditional Pueblo pottery makers or other American Indian potters in the United States and learn their techniques, or travel to Japan to watch the masters of Japanese pottery create their arts. There's also a travel trip to Japan where you study traditional influences on contemporary design in sculpture gardens and flower arranging. You can also join groups to explore beautiful gardens and their design in parts of the U.S. and abroad.

Other programs include the broad range of creative crafts such as weaving, quilt-making, batik, silkscreen, woodcarving, gem-carving and many more that reflect the variety of creative crafts in the world. At an Appalachian folk school, you can learn how to make a twig chair, put together a dazzling quilt, make your own banjo, watch a blacksmith create iron work, bake bread in a wood-fired stove, bind books, make a corn husk doll, or carve wood.

In Sedro Woolley, Washington you can learn drum-making at a workshop. In the Great Smoky Mountains, you can attend an arts center where students study wood turning, papermaking, stained glass, enameling and fabric painting among dozens of other programs. In California, you can join classes to learn jewelry making, silver smithing, and coiled basket making from Navajo, Hopi and Zuni artists.

One of the most unusual opportunities is a program on how to build your own house. The two-week course explains everything you need to know from the foundations up.

Crafts Organizations

Arrowmont School of Arts and Crafts
Art Trek
Augusta Heritage Center
Campbell Folk School
Canyonlands Field Institute
Centrum
Ciclismo Classico
Crow Canyon Archaeological Center
Cuisine International
Danu Enterprises
Dillman's Creative Art Workshops
Esprit Travel

Heartwood Home Building
Idyllwild Arts
North Cascades Institute
Journeys Into American Indian Territory
Smithsonian Study Tours
Spirit of India
TraveLearn
Tuscan Way
University of California-Berkeley
Wildland Adventures
Yellowstone Association Institute

LANGUAGE AND CULTURE

Bon jour! Guten tag! Buenos dias! Shalom! Sayonara!

A new language offers a window into another world. You not only learn words for "student," "umbrella," and "firehouse," but you are introduced to a new culture and another lifestyle through the language.

Eskimos have many words for snow, the Greeks have a vast vocabulary for the varieties of love, and the French and Italians have so many words related to food that they are recognized as international. A croissant is always a croissant and spaghetti needs no translation. You'll also find that "blue jeans" and "hamburgers" are now internationally recognized.

The most challenging and effective way to study a foreign language is to go to the country where it's spoken, and immerse yourself in the daily life. Somehow when you have to buy bread and no one speaks English, you'll learn what to request very quickly, and if you're hopelessly lost, you'll find out how to ask directions. It's an educational accomplishment as fascinating for older students as younger ones.

At first, you won't even be able to fathom the bus schedule or find your way along unfamiliar streets. But as the days pass and you realize you can find your way around, the language begins to sound quite normal. The people who looked alike turn into individuals, the words become recognizable, and your perspective moves from a critical comparison of what they're doing wrong to an open-minded appreciation of the differences.

Dozens of universities, colleges, and educational groups organize language courses abroad and expect that you will make a serious commitment to daily study and homework in order to gain the most benefit from the experience. The sense of achievement you will feel at the end is inspiring as you remember your first days.

A typical day begins with breakfast in a college cafeteria, a hotel or pension, or with your host family. You walk or bus to the school where classes usually start about eight or nine in the morning. Most courses offer four or five hours of instruction covering vocabulary, grammar, conversation, and pronunciation. Teachers are usually residents of the country and try to speak as little English as possible.

On the first day, students take a test to determine their level of ability. Classes are kept small and the pace is adapted to the group's abilities. There's usually a short mid-morning break.

When classes end, you may lunch at the school or with your host family, or on your own. There will be time during the day to study in the language labs using headphones and tapes, attend lectures on the culture and history of the country, or take extra classes. You will also have homework to prepare for the next day. Although there will be temptations to skip some of the work, your teachers will emphasize that in order to gain fluency in a new language, you should study and speak it as much as you can for the time you are there. Many programs offer a tour of the country as well as excursions to places of interest.

So what would you like to learn?

In Mexico, there are dozens of Spanish-language schools. Surprisingly, many of them are in Cuernavaca, a lovely city in the mountains about an hour's bus ride from Mexico City with plenty of inexpensive places to stay. In Guatemala, you can study Spanish, and in Spain you can find language courses in Seville, Madrid, Salamanca, Ovideo, and Pamplona, among other places.

You can learn French in Quebec, Canada, or cross the Atlantic to France to learn how they speak it in Paris, Besancon, Montpelier, Nimes, or Toulon, in the Pyrenees, in Normandy, and on the French Riviera among others.

There are German classes in Innsbruck, Hamburg, and Kassel. In Vienna, there are language courses and seminars on music. In Italy, you can study Italian in the medieval village of Poppi, or in Bologna, Turin, or Florence.

In Krakow, Lublin, and Warsaw you can study Polish. In Israel, there are intensive Hebrew courses where new immigrants and visiting foreigners learn the language. In Rio de

Janeiro, Brazil, you can study Portuguese. A Scandinavian program invites students of all ages, including Elderhostel participants, to live and study Swedish in Folk Colleges. Shanghai University offers a summer program of Chinese followed by a tour of the country. Other groups offer home-stays and Japanese-language programs in Tokyo.

Several companies can arrange for high-school students to spend part of a year abroad living with families in Australia, Italy, England, Spain, Japan, or Russia among other countries.

Language and Culture Organizations

British Studies at Oxford
Centro di Cultura Italiana in Casentino
Council on International Educational Exchange
Cross Cultural Journeys
Cuahnuhuac
Cuisine International
Danu Enterprises
Esprit Travel
French-American Exchange
Friends of Fiber Art International
Global Volunteers
International Bicycle Fund
International Expeditions
Journeys East
Journeys International
Kosciuszko Foundation
Mobility International
Myths and Mountains
National Registration Center for Study Abroad
Overseas Adventure Travel
Saga Holidays
Seniors Abroad International Homestay
Smithsonian Study Tours
Spirit of India
TraveLearn
Tuscan Way
University of California-Berkeley
University of New Orleans
University of Pennsylvania
University of Rhode Island
Wilderness Travel
World Learning

NATURE AND WILDLIFE

The natural world is shrinking. As people multiply, the rain-forest, wilderness areas, and untouched open spaces are taken over for houses and farmlands. More and more species are becoming extinct, disappearing forever from the face of the earth, and there is less and less wild land left without a human imprint.

For those who want to visit animals in their natural habitat and see the world as it was before man and civilization changed it, there are many opportunities available. Dozens of outstanding companies offer wonderful educational travel experiences that focus on animals and the environment, led by qualified naturalists and regional experts.

In the U.S., you can hike or horse pack through the magnificent canyons of the West, explore the coastal waters of Alaska in a kayak, or travel along the rivers that Lewis and Clark followed. You can see dramatic black and white orca whales off the coast of Washington's San Juan Islands or paddle along the Gulf of California in Baja and snorkel with incredibe fish.

In Africa, you can visit the Serengeti National Park with thousands of square miles of wilderness alive with lions, leopards, hyenas, cheetahs, giraffes, and more. Every year, the wildebeest and zebras migrate across the plains, an unforgettable sight as millions of animals in vast herds search for new grasslands. In Tanzania's Ngorongoro Crater, a deep natural amphitheater formed by the collapse of an extinct volcano, you can see unimaginable numbers of gazelles, hyenas, lions, elephants, and pink flamingoes.

In Kenya's Samburu Game Reserve, you may see rhinos, elephants, buffaloes, oryxes, giraffes, and rare species not often seen in the wild like the Somali ostrich, vulturine guinea fowl, and the leopard. In Rwanda, the home of mountain gorillas, you can seek the last of these shy, rare, and wonderful animals, living among the trees and scrub of the Akagera National Park. As your boat glides through the reed-filled waterways of the park, look for hippos and crocodiles.

In Nepal's Chitwan National Park, you can ride an elephant and look for Royal Bengal tigers, one-horned rhinos, spotted deer, wild boars, monkeys and leopards. And in Ecuador's Galapagos Islands, you can see huge tortoises a century old, blue-footed boobies on nests with their fluffy offspring, penguins, fur seals, playful sea lions, marine iguanas, pelicans, frigatebirds, and swallow-tailed gulls.

For a hands-on experience, you can volunteer to help save the sea turtles that come to the shore to lay their eggs. In North Carolina, researchers study the effects of the forest sanctuaries for black bears established in 1971. In Sarasota, Florida, you can assist studies of dolphins that focus on their social interactions. In Costa Rica, there's a project to study howler monkeys, while in Liberia, volunteers help research the distribution of chimpanzees in tropical rain forests.

Nature Organizations

Adventure Bound
AdventureWomen
Africa Travel Center
Alaska Wildland Adventures
American Horiticultural Society
American Museum of Natural History
Arctic Treks
Baja Discovery
Boojum Expeditions
Camp Denali & North Face Lodge
Canyonlands Field Institute
Country Inns Along the Trail
Denali Backcountry Lodge
Denali Wilderness Lodge
Denver Museum of Nature
    and Science
Dude Ranchers' Association
Echo: The Wilderness Company
Eldertreks
International Bicycle Fund
International Expeditions

Jams Henry River Journeys
Journeys
Journeys East
Lindblad Expeditions
Maine Windjammers Association
National Audubon Society
North Cascades Institute
Northern Lights Expeditions
Rocky Mountain River Tours
Sea Turtle Restoration project
Sea Quest Expeditions
Smithsonian Study Tours
Spirit of India
TraveLearn
The World Outdoors
UC Research Expeditions
Voyagers International
Wilderness Travel
Wildland Adventures
Yellowstone Association Institute

WATERWAYS

About two-thirds of our planet Earth is covered with water. To spend time exploring streams, rivers, lakes, and oceans on an educational trip afloat can provide a new perspective on land-bound lives.

Dozens of companies offer river-rafting trips on the rivers of Colorado, California, and other parts of the country through spectacular scenery and exciting white water. Today's modern lightweight rafts keep afloat on tossing waves and drift gently along on the river current between high canyon walls, low hills, or sandy shores edged with green trees, bushes, and unusual plants. You'll see fantastic vistas, night skies sparkling with stars, and enjoy a new view of the world from the water. Most companies offer a choice of a large raft powered by motor or oars, smaller rafts for about eight people where the group paddles, or rafts and kayaks for one or two people. There are schools that teach river-rafting skills, and exciting trips available in Costa Rica, Peru, India, China, Australia, or New Zealand.

There are tours along the Mississippi River on an old riverboat, where you lean over the deck and watch the towns flow by. Seeing Alaska from the water is an exciting way to travel there. You can take wilderness trips by yacht, canoe, or sea kayak, and there are excursions around Admiralty Island National Monument which has more brown bears and bald eagles than people. You can kayak on Alaskan fjords or Glacier Bay, or alongside Hubbard Glacier, and even join fishing trips and photography seminars.

Visit Antarctica and see its glaciers, icebergs, and penguins on a ship designed to break through ice. You live aboard and set out on day trips in Zodiac dinghies to see huge seals, bustling penguins, glaciers and ice floes, and spot birds unique to the frozen land.

In warmer waters, there are sea-kayak trips in Baja California where you paddle along the rocky coastline, camp on deserted sandy beaches, and dive for shellfish for dinner. You can also go down under to Australia for a sea-kayak trip on to the Great Barrier Reef to admire the coral shoals and vividly colored fish.

Cruise ships provide civilized tours with a little rocking on the waves. Elegant vessels offer gourmet meals, air conditioning, and luxury tours to Alaska, the Arctic, or Antarctic, to the coastal cities of the Mediterranean, up the Amazon and Orinoco Rivers of South America, up the Yangtze River in China, or along the romantic Danube in Europe. Most cruises carry experts aboard who present lectures, films, and informational seminars about the region.

Waterways Organizations

Adventure Bound River Expeditions
AdventureWomen
Alaska Wildland Adventures
American Horticultural Society
American Museum of Natural History
Arctic Treks
Baja Discovery
Camp Denali & North Face Lodge
Canyonlands Field Institute
Denver Museum of
   Nature and Science
Echo: The Wilderness Company
Eldertreks
International Expeditions
James Henry River Journeys
Journeys International

Lindblad Expeditions
National Audubon Society
National Trust for
   Historic Preservation
North Cascades Institute
Northern Lights Expeditions
Overseas Adventure Travel
River Travel Center
Rocky Mountain River Tours
Sea Quest Expeditions
Smithsonian Study Tours
The World Outdoors
Wilderness Travel
Wildland Adventures
Yellowstone Association Institute

SECTION 2:
ORGANIZATIONS

"Two roads diverged in a wood, and I —
took the one less traveled by,
And that has made all the difference."   Robert Frost

Adventure Bound River Expeditions

Contact: Tom & Robin Kleinschnitz
Address: 2392 H Road
            Grand Junction CO 81505
Phone: 970-245-5428
            800-423-4668
Fax: 970-241-5633
Email: ab@raft-colorado.com
Web: www.raft-colorado.com

Since 1963, Adventure Bound River Expeditions has offered trips through some of the most beautiful scenery in western America, designed for beginners and more experienced rafters and led by experienced raft guides.

One Ohio grandfather has taken annual trips with the company for 16 years, first taking his children, and now his grandchildren!

You can choose two, three, four, five or seven days of rafting down a variety of Colorado's rushing rivers. On the upper Green River the boats pass through the magnificent scenery of Desolation and Gray Canyons. Other trips float through Westwater Canyon or Horsethief and Ruby Canyons on the Colorado, along the Green River through Dinosaur National Monument, or down the Yampa, one of the last untouched major wild rivers that swells with spring run-off. The more challenging rapids are found in Cataract Canyon.

There's a choice of pontoon rafts, oar rafts, and paddle boats, and optional inflatable kayaks for those who want to try paddling on their own.

What you get: Camping accommodation, all meals, safety equipment, round trip transportation to and from Steamboat Springs or Grand Junction. Rental tents and sleeping bags available. Youth and group rates available.

What it costs:
$300 for 2 days, Westwater Canyon, Colorado River
$525 for 3 days, Lodore Canyon-Green River, Dinosaur National Monument
$810 for 5 days, Cataract Canyon-Colorado River, Canyonlands National Park

Rafting through exciting white-water rapids in Cataract Canyon

"I realized there was a measure of danger. Once faced and settled, there wasn't any good reason to refer to it."
Amelia Earhart.

AdventureWomen

Contact: Susan Eckert
Address: 15033 Kelly Canyon Road
Bozeman MT 59715
Phone: 406-587-3883
800-804-8686
Fax: 406-587-9449
Email: advwomen@aol.com
Web: www.adventurewomen.com

In 1982, when Susan Eckert started her company to introduce women over 30 to the outdoor world of hiking, traveling, rafting and exploring, she was told that the idea wouldn't work. Today she successfully offers dozens of adventure trips world-wide to active women over 30.

Susan Eckert finds that "women over 30 especially relish the freedom to be able to experience new things away from limiting societal expectations. They naturally create a non-competitive environment of support and encouragement for each other."

Trips run year round. Participants take winter ski trips in Montana or relaxing Baja visits to go sea kayaking and whale watching. In the spring there are trips down the Amazon River, an excursion to the fabled city of Machu Picchu, and an active journey through New Zealand that includes swimming with dolphins and glacier climbing.

Summer trips take women hiking in Europe, on a wildlife safari in East Africa, and on a hike to the Havasupai Indian Reservation at the bottom of the Grand Canyon in Arizona. There are also horseback trips in Montana and Iceland. A very popular trip is the week-long Montana Cowgirl Sampler, where you can ride a horse, hike, raft, and fish.

What you get: Round trip airfare on selected international trips, land transportation, accommodations, entry fees, excursions, guides, instructions, pre-trip material, reading lists, most meals. Special diets available.

What it costs:
$2,150 for 7 days, Rafting the Grand Canyon
$5,295 for 17 days, Nepal Himalaya Trek
$6,995 for 15 days, East African Wildlife Safari

Nepali woman and child

Africa Travel Center

Contact: Brian & Karen Cockburn
Address: PO Box 1918
Boulder CO 80306
Phone: 800-363-8024
303-473-0950
Fax: 303-546-0875
Email: info@africatvl.com
Web: www.africatvl.com

The Africa Travel Center specializes in creating African experiences through a variety of travel options including exclusive fly-in safaris, luxury tented safaris, overland camping adventures, walking safaris, canoe safari, and custom safaris to meet individual requirements.

Brian Cockburn a professional safari guide and wildlife biologist, was born and raised in Zimbabwe in southern Africa and has lived and traveled there extensively, and continues to lead safaris regularly. His wife Karen spent many years living in Africa and helps travelers and nature enthusiasts visit favorite places. They specialize in making sure every detail is taken care of, and can take you rafting, fishing, horseback riding, and game-viewing by foot, vehicle, and even elephant-back.

Their non-profit African Wildlife and Conservation Project (AWC) was created to provide a forum for information exchange among academics in wildlife biology, wildlife management, environmental studies, and natural resource management focusing on African environmental issues, to share information on current conservation projects in Africa, to address ecotourism and community based conservation, and to provide multimedia resources and an online database of research materials about Africa.

What you get: Accommodations, transportation incl. airfare in Africa, entry fees, excursions, guides, equipment, instruction, insurance, pre-trip materials, maps, reading lists, most meals. Special diets available.

What it costs:
$1,200 for 3 or more days, Horseback Safaris
$2,200 for 5 to 12 days, Walking Safaris
$4,200 for 12 days, Cultural Highlights, West Africa
$5,100 for 12 days, Family Safaris

"We looked a lioness in the eye, which chilled me down to my soul, had elephants peacefully moving through our camp in the moonlight, rode horses up to giraffes. All was wonderful." Participant on Horseback Safari

"Our friends on safari with us all agree that this was the most enjoyable, educational and rewarding experience that we ever had." Participant on Cultural Safari.

Alaska Wildland Adventures

Contact: Kirk Hoessle
Address: PO Box 389
          Girdwood AK 99587
Phone: 907-783-2928
          800-334-8730
Fax: 907-783-2130
Email: info@alaskawildland.com
Web: www.alaskawildland.com

"Consider pushing the edge just a bit," suggests director Kirk Hoessle. "Not too much, but just enough to be able to leave Alaska with its true essence - close encounters with wildlife, an appreciation for the harshness of this northern environment that helps keep this country wild, and the magic and realities of life in the Last Frontier."

A variety of Alaska adventures for families are offered by this experienced company which hopes that visitors to Alaska can experience the country first-hand with an expert guide, not just sightsee passively through the windows of a tour bus.

There's a choice of itineraries. You may raft the Kenai River and explore the Kenai National Wildlife Refuge and Skilak Lake. A boat tour shows you Kenai Fjords National Park where you see huge glaciers, sea otters, puffins, and seals. You flightsee over Mount McKinley. You tour Denali National Park to see caribou, grizzlies, and moose, and spend a day hiking and photographing in the park. You visit an Alaskan bush town.

You choose which accommodations you'd prefer on your tour: tent camping, cabin stays, a mixture of tent and cabin, or lodge and cabins. All trips visit remote and relatively natural environments and emphasize low impact travel. There's also a strong educational emphasis so that travelers learn about the natural and cultural history of the places they visit.

What you get: Accommodations, meals, transportation, activities, gear, equipment, full guide service.

What it costs:
$3,795 per adult/$3,495 per child 6-12, for 9 days, Alaska Family Safari
$4,895 for 11 days, Alaska Grand Safari

"For years we have yearned to visit Alaska. Now that our dream has been realized, we know that Alaska's greatest resource is the people who display an unbounded affection for the environment. The most fulfilling ten days we have experienced." Couple from New York.

American Horticultural Society

Contact: Leonard Haertter, Travel Planner AHS
Address: 7931 East Boulevard Drive
              Alexandria VA 22308
Phone: 800-942-6666
Fax: 314-721-8497
Email: lhh@haerttertravel.com
Web: www.haerttertravel.com

Visit beautiful gardens around the world with the American Horticultural Society Travel Study Program which offered its first tours in 1985. Participants are taken to visit private and public gardens accompanied by tour leaders and horticulturists who are experts in their field. Many of the private gardens are generally not open to the public. Most participants, who range in age from 35 to 95, are amateur or professional horticulturists.

The Society's headquarters in River Farm, one of George Washington's original farms, in Alexandria, Virginia, contains beautiful gardens as well as a wide variety of wildlife.

AHS garden tours explore the United States with visits to the lush gardens of Mississippi, the Canadian gardens of

Vancouver, and the coastal gardens of Maine. Other trips go abroad to see roses and hollyhocks in traditional gardens in England and to attend the Royal Chelsea Flower Show, and to see the gardens and castles of England, France, Wales and Ireland. In Italy, you tour the gardens of the Italian lakes, and visit others in Naples, Rome, and on the islands of Ischia and Capri. There are also trips to the gardens of China and India, and in South America, a tour of the gardens of the great houses and ranches of Argentina.

What you get: Transportation, accommodations, entry fees, excursions, guides, equipment, instruction, tips, pre-trip materials, reading lists, most meals.

What it costs:
$3,890 for 6 days, Coastal Gardens of Maine
$5,640 for 16 days, Gardens of China
$7,460-$11,660 for 10 days, Gardens of Coastal Iberia, France, Belgium
$300 tax-deductible donation to the AHS.

"The guide on our tour was superior — well informed and with extensive contacts. She made everyone feel comfortable and the entire tour was extremely well organized and carefully orchestrated." Texas couple who have taken several garden tours.

American Museum of Natural History

Contact: Julie Ann Kohn, Discovery Tours
Address: Central Park West at 79th Street
New York NY 10024-5192
Phone: 212-769-5700
800-462-8687
Fax: 212-769-5755
Email: discovery@amnh.org
Web: www.discoverytours.org

A pioneer in sponsoring educational and adventure tours, the Museum has been offering trips since 1953 and now runs dozens of expeditions to Antarctica, Alaska, Africa, Borneo, Europe, Russia, Nepal, and China among others. The tours provide a combination of study, adventure and leisure activities. Those who take the trips become Museum members.

Accompanying the trips are teams of lecturers from the Museum's extensive staff of scientists, as well as expert naturalists, astronomers, geologists, and art historians from leading universities and museums who provide informative programs along the way.

Travelers can explore Antarctica and the Falkland Islands, visit the tropical islands of Tahiti, join the first AMNH cruise to Cuba, sail up the Amazon and Orinoco Rivers of South America, take a family expedition to Alaska's glaciers, cruise the outer islands of Britain, Ireland and Scotland, see Patagonia's Towers of Paine, visit Tierra del Fuego, travel to the great temples of Southeast Asia, and follow the Elbe River from Prague to Berlin, join a private jet tour of the national parks of the American West, and tour gardens, temples and traditional culture in Japan among more than 60 trips.

Some trips are expeditionary, following the footsteps of past explorers who looked for the source of the Nile in Africa, and some are ground-breaking — trips to Cuba, Iran, and Saudi Arabia. Family programs include a Himalayan adventure in Nepal and a dinosaur dig in Colorado.

Because of their popularity, programs fill up quickly, so participants are advised to book early.

What you get: Accommodations, most meals, land transportation, excursions, baggage handling, transfers, guides, tips, entrance fees, education programs, pre-departure materials, insurance.

What it costs:
$1,350 to $2,600 for 7 days, Family Dinosaur Discovery
$5,595 to $6,495 for 14 days, Timbuktu and the Rivers of West Africa
$6,880 to $7,480 for 15 days, Papua New Guinea

Arctic Treks

Contact: Carol Kasza & Jim Campbell
Address: Box 73452
Fairbanks AK 99707
Phone: 907-455-6502
Fax: 907-455-6522
Email: arctreks@polarnet.com
Web: ArcticTrekAdventures.com

For more than 20 years, Arctic Treks has taken adventurous souls to experience one of the most remote and magnificent wilderness areas on the planet. As late as the 1930s, the area now known as Gates of the Arctic National Park was left as blank space on maps. Today, the region epitomizes the true, undeveloped wilderness; there are no roads, no trails, no campgrounds — only endless miles of wild mountains and rivers. It is part of Alaska's Brooks Range, some 700 miles long by 200 miles wide, and the northernmost extension of the Rocky Mountain chain.

Arctic Treks is a family-run operation. Carol Kasza, a former Colorado Outward Bound School instructor, has served as president of the Alaska Wilderness Guides Association. Both she and her partner Jim Campbell are trained in emergency medical care, and choose guides for their expertise in Arctic preservation. In 1999, the company won the World Wildlife Fund Arctic Award for Excellence in Linking Tourism and Conservation.

"We see our role as that of the friend you've found who has a wealth of contacts, knowledge, and information about this wild land" notes Carol Kasza.

In summer, when there is daylight all the time, some 14 trips are offered. You can go rafting on the headwaters of the Noatak, the largest untouched river basin in the United States, or down the Hulahula, named by homesick Hawaiians shanghaied to work on whaling ships at the turn of the century. You can also raft down the lower Kongakut River to the Arctic Ocean and along the coast to observe icebergs, seals, and rare Arctic seabirds. A fall caribou base camp offers the rare opportunity to watch hundreds of caribou make their way south across the land. Backpacking trips explore the Brooks Range where no trails, markers, or campsites show you which path to take across tussocks and bogs, often covered with bright wildflowers in June, and where moose browse in the willows while caribou and Dall sheep graze on the slopes.

What you get: Round trip airfare from Fairbanks, camping and cooking gear, food for all meals, Avon rafts, paddles, life jackets, guides, first aid and repair kits.

What it costs:
$1,875 for 7 days, Rafting Koyukuk North Fork
$2,450 for 7 days, Fall Caribou Base Camp
$3,075 for 10 days, Paddling the Arctic Coast

"This trip was one of the outstanding adventures of my life and I would jump at the chance to take another trip with you." Participant on hiking trip.

"People travel for the same reason as they collect works of art; because the best people do it." Aldous Huxley.

Arrowmont School of Arts and Crafts

Contact: Director
Address: PO Box 567/556 Parkway
Gatlinburg TN 37738-0567
Phone: 865-436-5860
Fax: 865-430-4101
Email: arrowmnt@aol.com
Web: www.arrowmont.org

The Arrowmont School is an internationally known visual arts complex that attracts more than 1,200 students every year. The curriculum includes landscape painting, drawing, basket weaving, wood turning, making wooden buckets and tubs, quilting, weaving, papermaking, photography, stained glass, silk-screening, fabric painting, stitchery, jewelry, enameling, and blacksmithing among others, taught by outstanding artists and specialists.

Arrowmont grew from a settlement school for young children in Gatlinburg, Tennessee, established in 1912 by a group of women to commemorate the founders of Pi Beta Phi, a national women's fraternity. The grateful children brought their teachers presents of handmade woven baskets and wooden carvings made by their parents. The beauty of the gifts so impressed the teachers that they established the Arrowcraft Shop in 1926 to sell local crafts. Today, thousands of tourists visit the shop.

The school attracts men and women of all abilities, ages, practical backgrounds, and educational achievement, who come from across the United States and abroad to attend one- and two-week sessions, special media conferences, seminars, community classes, and Elderhostel sessions.

Situated on 70 acres of wooded hillside near the Great Smoky Mountain National Park in Tennessee, the complex has large, well-equipped studios, a book and supply store with tools and materials for the courses, a resource center, an auditorium, and a gallery. Students live in simple furnished dormitory rooms in cottage-type buildings. Home-cooked meals are served in the communal diningroom.

What you get: Accommodations, all meals, tuition, facilities, activities.

What it costs:
$75 application fee. $280 for one week's tuition.
$205 to $470 for one week, room and all meals, Monday through Saturday breakfast, in dorm, shared room or cottage room.
$455 to $985 for two weeks, room, and all meals, plus four meals on Saturday and Sunday.
Additional materials fee for some classes. Scholarships available.

A Florida art teacher commented: *"Arrowmont has all the answers. It offers traditional crafts, but also is on top of what is contemporary. It's an oasis of fine crafts and good design."*

Art Trek

Contact: Carol Duchamp
Address: PO Box 1103
Bolinas CA 94924
Phone: 415-868-1836
888-522-2652
Fax: 415-868-9033
Email: carol@arttreks.com
Web: www.arttreks.com

Art Trek's hands-on art and travel workshops take artists to beautiful places in the United States and abroad to observe, paint and practice every day. Led by professional artists, the workshops explore a range of art techniques depending on the class, with instruction in careful observation, plein air composition, thumbnail sketching, mixing color, and creating form.

In Santa Fe and Taos, New Mexico, a drawing and watercolor workshop takes participants to paint American Indian pueblos, red rock canyons, and the region that Georgia O'Keeffe knew so well. Developing a visual journal is also included.

In Costa Rica, a drawing and watercolor workshop examines Rainforest as Landscape with visits to pristine rainforest settings along the Caribbean coast to see count-less flowers and hundreds of species of birds and butter-flies. Optional yoga and meditation classes are available.

In France, you study watercolor painting in the Dordogne region in the southwest, where the magnificent caves of Lascaux still hide 15,000-year-old paintings of horses, bison and deer. In the French Polynesian islands of Tahiti, Moorea, and Huahine, watercolor workshops focus on tropical flow-ers as well as the views of volcanic peaks, white-sand beaches, turquoise lagoons and breathtaking sunsets.

Founded in 1982, Art Trek aims to help artists develop a personal style and to provide individual technical assistance. Strategies for "freeing the artist" are always part of the pro-grams for beginners and experienced professionals. Classes have no more than 15 students.

What it costs:
$3,010 for 10 days, Drawing and Watercolor, New Mexico
$4,750 for 12 days, Tropical Flowers Watercolor, Tahiti
$5,630 for 15 days in Watercolor in New Ways, Dordogne, France

What you get: Roundtrip airfare, accommodations, trans-portation, some meals, excursions, guides, instruction, en-try fees, reading lists.

"Travel itself is like entering a dream life. Everything is changed and different. The shock of the new provides a dynamic context for feelings. Travelers often feel more alive, more engaged and mentally freed of the utilitarian focus required in everyday life. As a result, painting and artwork flourish." Carol Duchamp.

Ashokan Fiddle and Dance

Contact: Director
Address: 987, Route 28-A
West Hurley NY 12491
Phone: 845-338-2996

Set in the Catskill Mountains of New York State, the Ashokan Fiddle and Dance camp offers a series of one-week summer programs of music and dancing, and a chance to swim, canoe, walk the trails or just relax by the lake in a beautiful natural setting. The program is co-sponsored by the Office of Continuing Education at the State University of New York, College at New Paltz.

Every week you can join classes on Western and Swing, New England, French Canadian, English and Scandinavian, and Old Time, Appalachian and Cajun music and dance. You can try the Lindy and the jitterbug, doo-wop and scat singing, step dancing, quadrilles, or tap dancing. You can learn swing singing, percussion, mandolin playing, Cajun accordion, and old-time fiddle and banjo. The teachers come from around the country and are experts in their field.

"These programs are a meeting ground where people of all ages learn new skills, make new friends, and share good times in a secluded woodland setting," explains Jay Ungar, who, for more than 20 years has run the camp with Molly Mason. Both are resident musicians at Ashokan.

You can stay at campsites in a field or the forest, or in the bunkhouse with dormitory rooms. Excellent meals and late-night snacks are prepared by the resident chef. Only 175 people can attend each week so there are no facilities for part-time attendees or drop-in visitors. Early registration is recommended because the programs are very popular, and there's usually a waiting list.

What you get: Accommodations, all meals, classes, workshops.

What it costs: $555 per person. Work scholarships are available.

"I'll love you, dear, I'll love you
Till China and Africa meet
And the river jumps over the mountains
And the salmon sing in the street."   W. H. Auden

Augusta Heritage Center

Contact: Gordon Blackley
Davis & Elkins College
Address: 100 Sycamore Street
Elkins WV 26241-3996
Phone: 304-636-1903
Fax: 304-637-1317
Email: augusta@augustaheritage.com
Web: www.augustaheritage.com

Ever dream of playing blues guitar, crafting a quilt, or dancing Cajun style? Here's the place to learn, and to discover how to craft white oak baskets, make a mountain dulcimer, or build a stone wall.

The Augusta program started in 1973 as a means of passing on the crafts, music, dances and folklore traditions of Appalachia. Its name comes from the colonial era term for what is now this West Virginia region. Today, the Center serves as a focal point for a variety of projects including a state-wide Folk Arts Apprenticeship Program, the Augusta Heritage Records label, Elderhostel sessions, and more than 200 hands-on folk arts classes.

The summer Augusta Heritage Arts Workshops annually attract more than 2,000 people from across the country and around the world. Special Theme Week music classes highlight blues, Irish, Cajun, swing, guitar, bluegrass, dance, old-time, French-Canadian, and vocal music traditions.

In the evenings, there are concerts, jam sessions, storytelling programs, square dances, French Canadian, bluegrass and old-time dance, and craft demonstrations. The Augusta Festival in August includes evening concerts at Davis & Elkins College, a juried crafts fair, children's activities, and a public dance under the tall oak trees of Elkins City Park.

Classes take place on the wooded, 170-acre campus of Davis & Elkins College, about a five-hour drive west of Washington, D.C. The small, private liberal arts college is affiliated with the Presbyterian Church USA.

What you get: Accommodations, all meals. Tuition separate. Can stay off campus.

What it costs:
$345 for 7 days, tuition.
$273 for 7 days, on-campus semi-private room.

Baja Discovery

Contact: Karen Ivey
Address: PO Box 152257
San Diego CA 92195
Phone: 619-262-0700
800-829-2252
Email: bajadis@aol.com
Web: www.bajadiscovery.com

For more than 20 years, Baja Discovery has been introducing people to whales from a camp on the shores of San Ignacio Lagoon on the west coast of Baja California, Mexico.

Every winter pregnant gray whales arrive in the lagoon from the north to calve between mid-January and mid-March. When the babies are almost fully grown in the spring, they and their mothers swim the 6,000 miles back to Alaska for the summer. In 1976, local fishermen in the lagoon noticed that the gray whales began to come up to a fishing boat and waited to be touched and petted. Soon the word spread about the friendly whales.

Today, you chug out into the sheltered lagoon in a small Mexican motorized boat to wait for the whales to come and visit. With the motor running, you watch a huge gray mammal swim under the boat and comes up to the side so you can reach out and stroke the shiny gray skin. Sometimes a baby — as large as the boat — will show off with a spectacular leap out of the water right beside you. You can lean out of the boat and touch them — if they let you.

From the boat you see distant whales poke their heads up as they spy hop or leap out of the water in magnificent breaches. Ashore on quiet evenings you may hear the distant "whoosh" sounds of whales breathing as they float in the bay. The whole experience is astonishing.

With a special permit from the Mexican government, Baja Discovery's tented site overlooks the lagoon. Each tent has a cot, sheets, and sleeping bag. Outside are modern toilet facilities and solar showers. Meals include plenty of fresh fruit, vegetables, and seafood and are served in a large dining and activity tent. You can walk along shell-strewn beaches, and see night skies filled with dazzling stars.

In addition to the whale trips, the company offers a range of Baja natural history programs for people from eight to eighty. You can kayak to islands in the bay, join a week-long hiking trip, or choose special focus programs on birding and botany in Baja. All groups are kept small to preserve the environment.

What you get: Accommodations, airfare from San Diego or land transportation to camp, all meals, guides, equipment, excursions, instruction, pre-trip materials, reading lists. Special diets available.

What it costs:
$1,595 for 7 days, Wildlife on the Sea of Cortez
$1,825 for 7 days, Gray Whale Discovery
$700 to $1,750 for 4 to 8 days, Walk Baja Hiking

"It was terrific! An ocean view with a front porch to one of the most awesome, magical spectacles on earth. Where else can you lie on your cot with coffee in the morning and watch whales popping up to look at you?" Woman on Gray Whale Discovery tour.

Boojum Expeditions

Contact: M.C. Jenni
Address: 14543 Kelly Canyon Road
             Bozeman MT 59715
Phone: 406-587-0125
             800-287-0125
Fax: 406-587-3474
Email: boojum@boojum.com
Web: www.boojum.com

Horseback treks in Tibet, Mongolia, Argentina, Venezuela, Romania, and Yellowstone National Park are offered by this adventure company. In 1985, Linda Svendsen pioneered the first horseback riding trek into China's Inner Mongolia region. Today she and Kent Madin run Boojum Expeditions which offers trips that focus on the ancient horse-based cultures of Central Asia and the love of horses, riding, and adventure that characterizes those cultures.

Mongolia is where most of their trips are held, with treks to attend the annual horse festival, Naadam, and watch the races and competitions on the vast plains. Some trips also offer mountain biking, fly fishing, rafting, and trekking in addition to horse riding. The mountain-bike route follows dirt roads to Khovsgol National Park where you camp along the shores of Lake Khovsgol. Fly fishing takes you to four different rivers with camp and lodge based accommodations. On all trips, you have the opportunity to meet local people and sip tea with the nomadic herders.

In Tibet, the riding area is on the eastern Tibetan Plateau, annexed in the 1950s by China. The nomads of this region are renowned for their riding skill and fierceness in battle. Herds of yaks wander amid the lush, rolling highland plateau at 12,000 feet above sea level.

The Patagonia Horse Trek in Argentina begins in Bariloche south of Buenos Aires and explores Nahuel Haupi National Park with its spectacular mountain scenery while you ride spirited local horses on tours led by local gauchos. In Romania, a two-week itinerary combines horse riding in unspoiled Transylvania forests looking for bear, wolf, red deer and lynx, with hiking and four days of local sightseeing. There's also a winter ride along the peaceful beaches of Venezuela's Margarita Island, with sightseeing.

What you get: Accommodations, all meals, guides/ translators, in-country transportation including horses.

What it costs:
$3,350 for 16 days, Tibetan Highlands
$1,950 to $4,600 for 13 to 18 days, Mongolia

Advice from Linda Svendsen: *"You don't have be an expert rider but you must be willing to ride up to eight hours a day. We cover between 15 and 30 miles a day, often in very rugged terrain. There may well be days of riding in rain and wind, even snow. We camp with American backpacking style tents, meals are cooked by the local staff, and washing and bathroom facilities are what would be expected on a pack trip to the Rockies."*

Boulder Outdoor Survival School (BOSS)

Contact: Information Director
Address: PO Box 1590
Boulder CO 80306
Phone: 303-444-9779
800-335-7404
Fax: 303-442-7425
Email: info@boss-inc.com
Web: www.boss-inc.com

Teaching students how to do more with less and to live in harmony with the natural world, the Boulder Outdoor Survival School (BOSS) offers a variety of courses in the outdoors. People come to relearn the skills that their ancestors once mastered and used on a daily basis.

Founded in 1968, BOSS has been teaching traditional skills in Utah, Canada and Mexico to students from diverse backgrounds who want to test their physical and mental skills and see if they can "make it."

On Field Courses, students learn how to travel in the canyons of southern Utah for seven, 14, or 28 days with little more than a knife, a poncho, and a wool blanket. No modern backpacks, stoves, or sleeping bags are allowed. On all BOSS courses, students learn how to make cordage from plants, knives from river rocks, and shelters from the natural debris around them.

The company also offers Professional Development Programs for businesses, work groups, and teams that last from three to 14 days. These expeditions focus on leadership development, team building and problem solving skills. As well as many other relevant business topics, the intent of the program is to draw lessons from the experience that are applicable in today's work environment.

"People are intrigued with overcoming adversity against all odds. There is something fascinating about those who tolerate enormous hardships but are still able to come through and prevail," says Josh Bernstein, BOSS president.

What you get: Accommodations, all meals, instruction, permits, guides, excursions, transportation, pre-trip material.

What it costs:
$895 to $2,825 for 7 to 28 days, depending on course

British Studies at Oxford

Contact: Dr. Margaret B. Pigott
Address: 322 Wilson Hall at Oakland University
Rochester MI 48309-4401
Phone: 248-370-4131
Fax: 248-650-9107
Email: pigott@oakland.edu
Web: www.oakland.edu/oxford

A first-hand experience of British life and culture are offered through this program, which invites students to spend the summer at Oxford University in Oxford, England. Participants range in age from 18 to 85.

Lectures focus on authors and their books, trends in education, history, and politics among others. There are also visits to theaters, museums, historic cathedrals, archaeological sites, newspaper offices, business organizations, and the Houses of Parliament.

Participants live in Corpus Christi College, two blocks from the center of town. Meals are served in the Great Hall and morning coffee and afternoon tea in the Junior Common Room. Students have access to Oxford City Library and the College Library, both open 24 hours a day. They can also swim, play tennis or cricket, go jogging, biking or punting, browse in bookstores, visit local pubs, or explore the countryside nearby.

What you get: Accommodations, all meals, transportation, excursions, guides, instruction, entry fees, equipment, pre-trip materials, reading lists. Special diets available.

What it costs:
$3,250 including tuition, 3 weeks, Summer at Oxford.
$5,950 including tuition, 6 weeks, Summer at Oxford.

"On the Continent, people have good food; in England, people have good table manners."   George Mikes

Campbell Folk School

Contact: Director
Address: One Folk School Road
              Brasstown NC 28902
Phone: 828-837-2775
              800-365-5724
Fax: 828-837-8637
Email: maryw@folkschool.org
Web: www.folkschool.org

Hundreds of weekend and week-long classes in culture, history and art are offered by the John C. Campbell Folk School, founded in 1925. This unique collaboration between progressive educators inspired by the Folk Schools of rural Denmark and the people of the southern Appalachian community of Brasstown in North Carolina brings together students and teachers to learn traditional skills. The campus has a History Center with a display on life in 20th century Appalachia and a craft shop featuring the selected works of more than 300 artists.

The School, set in 380 acres of rolling farmland, is open year-round and offers an amazing variety in its 450 classes. You can make your own banjo, fire and bend steel into artistic ironwork, or discover the joy of contra dancing. You can build a twig chair, learn to carve a piece of wood, or perfect the skill of turning a wooden bowl. You can learn how to cook home-baked bread in a wood-fired stone hearth, plan an heirloom garden, and learn the uses of medicinal herbs. Music instruction teaches you how to play the guitar, banjo, dulcimer or fiddle. There are classes in crochet, papermaking, bookbinding, corn husk doll making, spinning and dyeing, stained glass, jewelry making, knitting, bobbin lace techniques, quilting, rug weaving and hooking, weaving, and many more. The teachers come from around the country and have outstanding credentials as experts in their fields.

Classes run for a week, five days, or a weekend. You can attend free concerts every Friday, community folk dances every other Saturday, and informal performances by folk musicians and storytellers. The dining-room serves three meals a day, and serves its famous fresh-baked bread.

What you get: Tuition. Class materials extra.
You book accommodations and all meals in dorms, private rooms with shared baths, and private rooms with private baths. The Folk School campground is also available but meals are optional for those camping. Call the School for more information.

What it costs:
$294 for 6 nights, week-long classes, tuition only.
$268 for 5 nights, five-night classes, tuition only.
$168 for weekend classes, tuition only.

Camp Denali & North Face Lodge

Contact: Jerryne Cole
Address: PO Box 67
Denali National Park AK 99755
Phone: 907-683-2290
Email: info@campdenali.com
Web: www.campdenali.com

Set in the heart of Alaska's 5.7 million acre Denali National Park and Preserve with a spectacular view of Mount McKinley are two small wilderness lodges. Visits here emphasize the natural and cultural history of the far north through active learning vacations that focus on naturalist-guided hiking and wildlife observation. Between June and September guests enjoy a summer wilderness experience far different from the hectic tempo of modern living.

Guests are met at the park entrance by a driver-naturalist and taken on an 89-mile northern safari into the heart of Denali where grizzly bears, Dall sheep, caribou, and moose roam unmolested. Along the way they learn about the geology of the Alaska Range, the cultural history of interior Alaska, and the park's birds, mammals, and alpine wildflowers.

Camp Denali integrates a rustic atmosphere with the solitude of wilderness living. Spread out over a tundra hillside, about 35 guests live in private cabins with a central shower facility, dining room and living room building. There's also a natural history resource center, a reference library, and a Special Emphasis series with guest lecturers who include nature writers, photographers and historians. Minimum stays are three or four nights.

North Face Lodge, a rambling single storey building, has the ambiance of a small country inn with 15 modern guest rooms, a living and dining room. Minimum stays are three or four nights.

What you get: Accommodations, all meals, land transportation, entry fees, excursions, guides, equipment, instruction, pre-trip material, reading lists. Special diets available.

What it costs:
$345 per person per night, plus tax

North Face Lodge and Mount McKinley, Alaska

Canyonlands Field Institute

Contact: Registrar
Address: PO Box 68
Moab UT 84532
Phone: 435-259-7750
800-860-5262
Email: cfiinfo@canyonlandsfieldinst.org
Web: www.canyonlandsfieldinst.org

The starkly dramatic region of the Canyonlands lies in the heart of the Colorado Plateau of southeastern Utah, close to Arches National Park and Canyonlands National Park and near the canyons of the Colorado and Green Rivers.

The Canyonlands Field Institute was created in 1984 "to promote understanding and appreciation of the natural and cultural heritage of the Colorado Plateau region through seminars for adults and students." It offers individuals the opportunity to learn about the Colorado Plateau with friends and family, and with others of all ages who share their interests.

CFI field-oriented seminars last from a day to a week and are led by guest experts. Topics covered include the lizards of Arches National Park, dinosaur tracking, literary landscapes of Canyonlands, teacher workshops, writing workshops, and a spring Eagle Float river trip looking for eagles nesting along the river. In addition, you can join river trips on the Green, Colorado, San Juan, and Dolores Rivers, and overnight hiking trips with pack stock support that explore the canyons.

CFI also organizes a number of Elderhostel programs each year. Summer camps for children include river skills workshops and ecology land trips. Custom programs for groups of all ages are available. CFI's field camp makes a great place to hold a family reunion or retreat.

What you get: Some accommodations, most meals, guides, equipment, instruction, reading lists, and some transportation. Tee-shirts on multi-day trips. Vegetarian diets available.

What it costs:
$50 for one day guided tours
$80 for one day river trip, Eagle Float
$130 for multi-day river trips per day per adult
Discounts for CFI members and youth under 18.

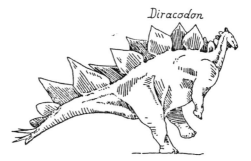

Diracodon

Centro di Cultura Italiana in Casentino

Contact: Stephen Casale
Address: One University Place/Apt 17-R
New York NY 10003-4522
Phone: 212-228-9273
Email: stevec@inch.com
Web: www.studyabroad.com/ccic

In the northeastern part of Tuscany in Italy, between Florence and Arezzo, is the medieval town of Poppi. It sits atop a hill above rolling valleys, the square tower of its dramatic castle visible for miles around. Poppi is ideally suited for those who wish to see the work of Piero della Francesca and other Renaissance artists in churches and museums nearby.

The Centro di Cultura Italiana Casentino was founded in 1980 in collaboration with the town and offers intensive Italian language courses. Classes run for two or four weeks between April and October. There are four hours of instruction every morning Monday through Friday, followed by visits to historic sights in the afternoons.

Several times a week students, teachers, and other Italian friends dine together at various restaurants in the region, enjoying Tuscan cuisine with home-made pasta, fresh vegetables, and salads. Students stay in furnished apartments that have been set aside for them by the school, or they can stay with Italian families, or in a country house near Poppi.

Students can also swim, horse ride, hike, or play golf, volleyball, tennis, or basketball. Almost every weekend, there are village festivals, such as the feast of the *porcino* mushroom, when everyone celebrates with food, drink, music, and dancing in the piazza.

What you get: Accommodations, some meals, tuition, activities, excursions. Prices are approximate: tuition is paid in Italian currency.

What it costs:
$1,000 per person, for 2 weeks.
$1,800 per person, for 4 weeks.

"Whoever wants to really study Italian and at the same time get to know the country and its people will find the CCIC the perfect place to do it." A participant.

"They spell it Vinci and pronounce it Vinchy; foreigners always spell better than they pronounce." Mark Twain

Centrum Summer Arts

Contact: Tracy Thompson
Address: Fort Worden State Park
PO Box 1158
Port Townsend WA 98368
Phone: 360-385-3102
800-385-3102
Fax: 360-385-2470
Email: tracy@centrum.org
Web: www.centrum.org

Centrum, about 50 miles from downtown Seattle, was established in 1973 as a non-profit center for the arts and education, and presents visual, literary, and performing arts to the public.

Located at Fort Worden State Park Conference Center in Port Townsend, Washington, and housed in what was once a military fort, it has a 1,200-seat theater, the McCurdy Pavilion (which served as a balloon hangar in the World War I), a Marine Science Center, a print studio, and several rehearsal spaces. There are ample opportunities to go sailing, kayaking and walking on the miles of forested hillside trails around the park, with stunning views of the Olympic Mountains in the distance.

Centrum offers month-long creative residencies for artists as well as performances by musicians and dancers in workshops and festivals. Attracting classical, jazz, blues, traditional, and popular musicians, there's a variety of events you can attend in the summer including a blues festival, an American fiddle tunes festival, Jazz Port Townsend, symphony concerts, and the Pacific Northwest Ballet. Most performances are preceded by week-long workshops. In July, there is a 10-day Writers Workshop.

What you get: Tuition only. Dormitory rooms (rent linens for $15 a week) and meal service available for about $200 per week. Housing list on request.

What it costs:
$285 for 7 days, Festival of American Fiddle Tunes.
$300 for 6 days, Blues Workshop.
$475 for 7 days, Jazz Workshop.

"It's wonderful to make merry with music. A great frolic. New musical ideas help to warm one during the cold times." A participant in Fiddle Tunes program.

Ciclismo Classico

Contact: Lauren Hefferon
Address: 30 Marathon Street
Arlington MA 02472
Phone: 781-646-3377
800-866-7314
Fax: 781-641-1512
Email: info@ciclismoclassico.com
Web: www.ciclismoclassico.com

Lauren Hefferon founded her company in 1988 "with the dream of creating culturally enriching, spectacular, and active itineraries throughout Italy." Today, she offers 25 exciting bike and hike tours that celebrate Italian landscape, art, language, music, folklore, and cuisine.

Bicycle trips are rated for beginners who like a meandering pace, athletic beginners who are energetic and like a challenge, intermediates who train regularly, and advanced riders who are avid cyclists. Groups are kept small, and there is a support van.

Hiking trips are rated in the same way, and groups are usually fewer than 12. The hiking trips are interspersed with cooking demonstrations, Italian lessons, and lectures given by expert natives on such topics as architecture, history, nature, art, or wine making. In addition, hikers visit festivals, artists' studios, musical events, cheese or oil-making demonstrations, and enjoy lunch with members of Lauren's extended family and friends.

One ride goes across Italy from the waters of the Adriatic to the Mediterranean Sea through Umbria and Tuscany, past fields of red poppies, and orchards filled with the aromas of lemon, olive, and fig. Another travels from Venice to Bologna with cycling along canals, a visit to Ravenna and its treasures of Byzantine art, and a ride through orchards laden with fruit to Faenza, a ceramics center.

Hiking trips explore the Italian and Swiss Alps and lakes, villages along the steep shore of Cinque Terre, and the island of Sicily and the nearby Aeolian Islands. There's also a cross-country skiing trip in the northern Dolomite mountains and a stay in Cortina, host to the 1956 winter Olympics, with horse-drawn sleigh rides, a visit to local woodworkers, and a wine and grappa tasting.

What you get: Accommodations, most meals, snacks and drinks, guides, equipment, pre-trip material, reading lists, route maps, excursions, transportation, cycle clinics. Bike rentals available. Bring helmets.

What it costs:
$2,495 for 8 days, Sicily's Ancient Pathways
$2,595 for 8 days, Tuscan Fantasy
$3,195 for 6 or 9 days, Venice to Bologna

"Ciclismo Classico provides so much more than a tour. Absorbing the region's culture is a treat. You always introduce me to new Italian customs, arts, history and culture. Thank you!" Participant from Colorado.

Council on International Educational Exchange

Council Exchanges
Address: 633 Third Avenue, 20th floor
New York NY 10017-6706
Phone: 1-888-COUNCIL
Email: info@councilexchanges.org
Web: www.councilexchanges.org

Council-International Study Programs
Address: 633 Third Avenue, 20th floor,
New York NY 10017
Phone: 1-800-40-STUDY
Web: www.ciee.org/study

Council Travel
Address: Visit our website for office locations
Phone: 1-800-2COUNCIL
Email: info@counciltravel.com
Web: www.counciltravel.com

There are three divisions of CIEE, a large private, not-for-profit membership organization that develops, facilitates, and administers international educational travel programs throughout the world. Established in 1947, Council Exchanges develop programs for work exchanges that help young people gain international perspectives and cross-cultural fluency. You can work abroad for four months in Australia or six other countries, teach English in China, or volunteer in one of the thousands of programs that last between two and four weeks in more than 25 countries.

The International Study Programs offer a different experience. You choose an academic program in one of 25 countries and live and study abroad for a semester or longer.

The third division of CIEE is Council Travel, one of the largest budget travel organizations in the U.S. with more than 65 centers. Council Travel has helped millions of travelers with their plans. CIEE's annual *Student Travel Catalog* provides essential information about travel, work, and study abroad programs, as well as with voluntary service opportunities.

The Council's mission is to help people gain understanding, acquire knowledge, and develop skills for living in a globally interdependent and culturally diverse world, and, notes a CIEE representative, "in an ever-expanding global economy, the maturity and independence gained in an international experience can put you a step ahead of others candidates in a job search, and will boost your self-esteem and confidence."

What you get: Tuition, housing, all meals, orientation, cultural activities, local excursions, field trips, pre-departure advising, insurance, International Student Identity Card. Facilities vary depending on location.

What it costs:
$2,100 for 6 weeks, summer, Technical University, Turkey
$7,950 for spring semester, Budapest University, Hungary
$5,600 for fall semester, tuition only, Anglia Polytechnic University, Cambridge, England

Country Inns Along the Trail

Contact: Director
Address: 843 Van Cortland Road
             Brandon VT 05733-8896
Phone: 800-838-3301
             802-247-3300
Fax: 802-247-6851
Email: office@inntoinn.com
Web: www.inntoinn.com

Learn about Vermont on self-guided and guided hiking, biking, and cross-country ski vacations with overnights in charming country inns with this company that's been offering such trips for 26 years. The trails follow famous hiking paths, such as the Long Trail that runs the length of Vermont and and other backwoods trails. The inns are carefully chosen for their superb hospitality.

Every inn has its own distinct character. Churchill House has antique furnishings and an eclectic international menu. Blueberry Hill is a restored 1813 farmhouse with 12 guest rooms and gourmet cuisine. Chipman Inn is a small 1828 country inn and the Tulip Tree is renowned for its backwoods luxury. All have comfortable guest rooms with private bath, common rooms, country views and a relaxing atmosphere.

The self-guided hikes use car shuttles to the trail each morning, and you drive your car to the trail end where you find at the end of a day's hiking ready to drive to the next inn. You need only carry a daypack for hiking with lunch and essentials and your luggage stays in the car.

The self-guided bicycling trips are designed for cyclists who want luggage transported between inns but don't need a leader. All trips begin and end in Brandon where you leave your car. You cycle through rolling farmlands and lush forested valleys, along quiet roads and unspoiled countryside, and stay at country inns at night.

Guided hike and bike trips cover the same area but with friendly local guides to show you the way. Most trips are for five nights. In the winter there are self-guided ski-touring trips along the Catamount Trail from inn to inn in Vermont's Green Mountains.

The company also offers guided walking trips in Maine, and abroad in England and Wales.

What you get: Accommodations, dinner, breakfast, trail lunch, taxes, inn gratuities, guide service, tours, entrance fees, transportation shuttle. Trip plan and maps on self-guided trips.

What it costs:
$335 for 3 nights, per person, double room, Heart of Vermont, bike/hike.
$530 for 4 nights, per person, double room, Hiking Gourmet.
$995 for 8 nights, per person, double room, Hiking Long Trail.

"The Inn-to-Inn is simply the best combination of hiking and vacationing we have ever experienced." Participant on Long Trail hike.

Cross Country International Equestrian Vacations

Contact: Information
Address: PO Box 1170
              Millbrook, NY 12545
Phone: 800-828-8768
Fax: 914-677-6077
Email: xcintl@aol.com
Web: www.equestrianvacations.com/cci_toc.html

For a different learning perspective on your travels, take a horse riding trip where you'll meet other horse lovers, friendly people united by interest and experience. CCI specializes in trail rides abroad and residential riding camps. Choose from vacations in Ireland, England, France, and Scotland as well as Spain, Italy, and Costa Rica.

Among the rides in Ireland is one in the southwest, in Killarney, on the Ring of Kerry Trail with stays at b&bs along the way. You explore the McGillicuddy Reeks, the highest Irish mountain range, country lanes and mountain tracks, and enjoy a four-mile ride on golden sands.

In England, you explore the Devon Moors. You stay at Higher Chilcott Farm in Exmoor and enjoy day rides through ancient pine forests, along the Danesbrook River, across Vernford Moors with breathtaking views, and see the famous Exmoor ponies.

In France, there's an inn to inn ride in Provence, which starts in the foothills of the Luberon Mountain Range near the village of Lauris. You ride along paths with views of the blue Mediterranean Sea to the south and to the Alps to the north, follow old Roman roads, see ancient castles, ride through flowering lavender and heather, pass herds of sheep with bells, and enjoy views of chestnut trees. Delicious picnics of Provencal cuisine are served along the way.

You can also choose vacations at riding centers that offer hunt seat, cross country and dressage training instruction in Wales, Ireland, France, England, and Millbrook, N.Y. There are young people's riding camps in Wales and Ireland, and a chance to go fox or stag hunting in Ireland and England.

What you get: Accommodations, all or most meals, horse, tack, guide, luggage transfer, tax, sightseeing, pre-trip material. Varies with ride.

What it costs:
$1,095 for 7 nights, Killarney ride, Ireland
$1,350 for 7 nights, Exmoor ride, England
$1,450 for 6 nights, South of France ride

Cross Cultural Journeys

Contact: Carole Angermeir
Address: PO Box 907
Mill Valley CA 94942
Phone: 415-380-8018
800-353-2276
Email: cat@well.com
Web: www.crosculturaljourneys.com

"We believe there are two aspects to any journey — the outward physical one, often to a new and exotic location, and the inward journey you take when you leave all that is familiar and allow new experiences, people, places, and customs to touch you and be your teacher," explains Carol Angermeir, president of Cross Cultural Journeys.

Since 1991, her educational programs explore cultures, offer trips on special themes, and journeys to discover belief systems. In Tibet and Nepal you trek to beautiful Mount Kailash, the center of the Hindu universe, and trek round it in a clockwise direction. It takes three days but you see devout pilgrims who spend weeks on the journey bowing and prostrating themselves on the ground.

In Bhutan, the tiny Buddhist kingdom in the Himalayas, you arrive when the world-renowned sacred Tantric dance festival takes place, and pilgrims from every part of the region attend. In contrast, in the lush highlands of Bali, you stay at a mountain resort with time for quiet meditation at a lakeside temple and enjoy local dance and gamelan music.

A journey to Cuba has as its focus the interconnected worlds of Cuban music and Santeria religion where you dance at salsa clubs and meet musicians, and also visit Santeria priests and take part in exotic rituals and ceremonies. You can also join Vision Quest trips in the Sierra Nevada of California and in Utah's canyonlands.

A new program, Special Crossroads Journeys, led by a former diplomat, travel to Northern Ireland, Cuba, Morocco and South Africa to explore societies that are at social, political, or economic crossroads.

What you get: Airfare from U.S., local flights, accommodations, all meals, transportation, entry fees, excursions, guides, equipment, instruction, tips, pre-trip material, reading lists. Special diets available. Educational leader and theme for each trip.

What it costs:
$1,500 for 7 nights, Mountain Vision Quest
$3,690 for 8 nights, Cuba
$4,590 for 15 nights, Southern India
$6,890 for 26 nights, Tibet and Nepal

"The trip truly transformed my life. It has given me depths of understanding, consciousness and a beautiful spiritual perspective that I don't think I could have found anywhere else." Participant on Peru trip.

Crow Canyon
Archaeological Center

Contact: Information Director
Address: 23390 Country Road K
             Cortez CO 81321
Phone: 970-565-8975
             800-422-8975
Fax: 970-565-4859
Email: marketing@crowcanyon.org
Web: www.crowcanyon.org

The archaeologists at Crow Canyon Archaeological Center are dedicated to long-term research on the ancestral Puebloan occupation of the Mesa Verde region. For reasons no one has yet completely understood, the 10,000 people who were living on and around the Mesa Verde Plateau in Southwestern Colorado at the beginning of the 12th century abandoned their homes and settlement and left the Mesa Verde region by the year 1300. A complex farming culture vanished from a hauntingly beautiful land where it had flourished for more than a thousand years. Those ancient people left no written account of their remarkable stay, but they did leave behind deserted communities built of stone and filled with the items of daily life.

Throughout the year, thousands of people come to work with archaeologists amid the mesas, mountains, and canyons, helping to contribute to innovative archaeological research and educational knowledge at Crow Canyon. Anyone can become a participant in the nationally acclaimed adult excavation program. You work alongside some of the finest research archaeologists in the Southwest to help excavate ancestral Pueblo Indian sites and later, spend time in the lab helping to analyze and interpret artifacts such as pottery and stone tools.

In addition to the archaeology programs, Cultural Explorations explores remote and seldom visited sites in the area on programs led by noted scholars and local experts. These trips include hiking, biking and horseback riding adventures, workshops in pottery and music, and excursions elsewhere in the Southwest, and to Alaska, and abroad to Central America, Egypt, Turkey, India, and Africa.

Crow Canyon also offers exciting hands-on education programs for school groups from March to November as well as summer programs for teens.

What you get: Tuition, accommodations, all or most meals, transportation, excursions.

What it costs:
$700 to $900 for 7 days, Adult Research Program.
$1,095 to $1,895 for 7 days, Explorations of American Southwest
$725 to $2,500, one week to one month, Summer Programs for Teens

Cuauhnahuac

Contact: Marcia Snell, U.S. Representative,
Address: 519 Park Drive
Kenilworth IL 60043
Phone: 847-256-7570
800-245-9335
Fax: 847-256-9475

Cuauhnahuac is the original name for Cuernavaca in Mexico, where this language institute, founded in 1972, offers intensive programs in the Spanish language and Mexican culture. Credit affiliation is with Northeastern Illinois University and University of La Verne in Illinois.

Class size is limited to four students and there are six hours of classroom instruction daily. Every day there are three hours of grammar, an hour and a half of conversation, and workshops in writing, pronunciation, reading, idiomatic expressions, and Mexican singing and dancing. There are also classes on Mexican history, literature, art, education, geography, Indian cultures, society, and politics. The full course runs for 12 to 16 weeks, but students can sign up for shorter periods. Classes begin every week at all levels.

The instructors, all Mexicans, speak only Spanish during classes. Private instruction on an individual basis is available.

The Institute offers personal attention and flexibility in order to meet each student's individual needs, and special classes for people in different professions can be arranged. Students can join trips to the Xochicalco pyramids, the colonial town of Taxco, and to Tepotzlan, an Indian village.

Cuauhnahuac is housed in a colonial building with classrooms, library, recreation room, lecture hall, a spacious garden, a swimming pool, and a volleyball court. An independently operated restaurant provides food. Students come from all over the world and include teachers, diplomats, and retirees. Most live with Mexican families recommended by the Institute.

What you get: Accommodations with Mexican family, all meals, tuition. Registration fee $70.

What it costs:
$18 per person per night, shared room.
$28 per person per night, private room.
$200 for 7 days, tuition.
$680 for 28 days, tuition.

"Not only is this the best way to learn Spanish, but it's a great vacation as well." Participant from Illinois.

Cuisine International

Contact: Judy Ebrey
Address: PO Box 25228
Dallas TX 75225
Phone: 214-373-1161
Fax: 214-373-1162
Email: CuisineInt@aol.com
Web: www.cuisineinternational.com

Sipping wine on a balcony overlooking the azure blue waters of the Neopolitan Riviera or sitting in a garden admiring the rolling French countryside near Bordeaux are among the beautiful settings for cooking classes where you cook — and eat — with the experts.

Cuisine International was founded by Judy Ebrey in 1987 and she now represents 18 week-long cooking schools and culinary experiences throughout the Western world. The business is family run by Judy, her husband, Richard Ebrey, Judy's son Craig Terrell, and his wife Amy. Each school is personally visited before inclusion. The majority of them are in Italy and France.

Amalfi, Italy

The historic town of Amalfi hugs the coast of the Italian Riviera below steep rugged hills. Classes are given in the Saracen Tower overlooking the bay and you stay in the Luna Convento Hotel which is carved out of the mountainside.

Chef Enrico Franzese and school director Rosemary Anastasio introduce you to the secrets of southern Italian cuisine, considered to be one of the healthiest diets in the world, using the colorful vegetables of the Mediterranean, fresh seafood, and pasta. After classes in the morning, the menu prepared is served for lunch.

There are excursions to walk round Amalfi, a trip to Sorrento, and a guided tour to Pompeii. In the evenings you enjoy gourmet dinners prepared by Enrico or go to superb local restaurants.

Bordeaux, France

In the countryside outside the port city of Bordeaux, France, is the Domaine D'Esperance, the 18th century home of le Comtesse J. L. de Montesquiou Fezensac, surrounded by vineyards and the rolling hills of Gascony. You stay in one of the comfortable guest rooms in the house.

Chef Natalia Arizmendi, who holds a Grande Diplome of the Cordon Bleu, offers one-week seminars six times a year for only nine students at a time. Each morning is devoted to theoretical instruction; in the afternoon you gain practical experience preparing the evening meal under her supervision. Chef Natalia has been teaching cooking and pastry for more than ten years.

On Wednesday morning you visit the local food market and on Saturday tour the wine cellars in the neighborhood. There's also time to walk along wooded paths, take a swim in the pool, or taste the homemade Armagnac from the Domaine's cellars.

Cuisine International (continued)
Other Schools

The company also has schools in Brazil and Portugal, and a school in England near Oxford owned by French chef Raymond Blanc.

What you get: Accommodations, entry fees, excursions, guides, instruction, most meals.

What it costs:
$2,700 to $3,000 for 7 days, Italy
$1,750 to $1,950 for 5 days, France

"It was one of the very best trips and experiences I have ever had! The classes went way beyond my expectations. Enrico has such a passion for cooking." Woman from Texas at Amalfi, Italy.

"We could not have imagined a more enjoyable time. Natalia is a marvelous chef as well as a wonderful person." Couple from Ohio at Bordeaux, France.

Danu Enterprises

Contact: Judy Slattum
Address: PO Box 156
Capitola CA 95010
Phone: 831-476-0543
888-476-0543
Email: danu@earthlink.net
Web: www.danutours.com

Specializing in artistic and spiritual tours to Bali, the company is named for the Balinese Hindu Goddess of Lakes and Streams because "we are continually in motion, evolving and meandering to encompass the newest and most compelling aspects of educational and adventure travel," says company director Judy Slattum.

Experiencing the Arts in Bali began in 1979 and is based in Ubud, the cultural center of the island. The trip offers classes in gamelan music, dance, painting, batik, or mask carving, all taught by Balinese artists who work in their family compounds. It is designed for artists, teachers, and those who appreciate art and culture.

Other trips to Bali explore the traditional healing arts and visits folk doctors to study herbal medicines, temple offer-

A wedding celebration in Bali

Judy Slattum

ings, yoga, and meditation. A culinary trip investigates Balinese food and visits rice fields, coffee and clove plantations, palm wine making, turtle breeding farms, as well as native cooking classes. A new active adventure trip goes trekking to volcanoes, jungle forests, native villages and monuments, and includes snorkeling.

There are also tours to the Greek Islands that focus on the ancient Minoan and Mycean cultures and include a five-day tour of the Peloponnese to see the temple of Apollo at Delphi and the palaces of Mycenae. In Italy, there's a February tour of Carnival in Venice with trips to Verona and Sardinia to join their annual celebrations, and an arts tour of the Tuscany region with visits to Florence, Lucca, and Siena where classes in stained glass, antique furniture restoration. and wallpaper, ceramics, or classical painting are offered.

What you get: Airfare from U.S., transportation, accommodations, entry fees, excursions, guides, instruction, pre-trip material, reading list, some meals. Special diets available.

What it costs:
$2,750 to $2,850 for 14 days, Back Roads of Bali
$3,100 to $3,500 for 23 days, Experiencing the Arts in Bali
$3,500 for 21 days, Greek Islands

"Your knowledge, experience, kindness, patience and humor made the trip for me. My classes were fun but challenging — I learned so much and this trip far exceeds what I could have hoped for. I shall return to Bali." Participant from Florida on Bali Arts trip.

"I'll remember the beautiful views of the blue Aegean Sea in Santorini, the wonderful little side streets of Chania, the cool swim after the hike through the Samaria Gorge, and all the great meals." Participant from California on Greek Islands trip.

Denali Backcountry Lodge

Contact:	Rebecca Downey
Address:	PO Box 810
	Girdwood AK 99587
Phone:	907-783-1342
	800-841-0692
Fax:	907-783-1308
Email:	info@denalilodge.com
Web:	www.denalilodge.com

Situated deep within Alaska's Denali National Park, in the Kantishna region at the end of the restricted use park road, is Denali Backcountry Lodge, set along the bank of Moose Creek.

Kantishna was a goldmining district at the turn of the century, but mining is now limited since the area was included in the park.

Your stay includes a narrated drive to the lodge which takes about five hours with plenty of time for photographing wildlife. When you arrive, you find 30 cedar cabins and a spacious main building complete with dining and lounge areas. Every cabin is heated and has two beds and a private bath.

You'll find comfortable accommodations, home-style meals, and adventurous options for exploring the park. You can be as active as you want. Join a hike to explore nearby ridges. See the dramatic peaks of Mount McKinley (Denali) if the weather is clear. Try mountain biking, enjoy flightseeing, evening programs, and even gold panning to glimpse the lifestyle of early settlers. In addition to the daytime naturalist-led programs, there are also presentations in the evenings.

The lodge is open from June through September.

What you get: Transportation to and from Park entrance with narrated wildlife search, all meals and snacks, all guided activities except flightseeing, all naturalist programs, park entrance fees.

What it costs:
$280 per person per night, four in cabin.
$305 per person per night, three in cabin.
$330 per person per night, two in cabin.
Recommended minimum 3 nights stay.
Reservations accepted up to a year in advance.

"Thank you all for a very enjoyable, educational, comfortable, fun and delicious stay at Denali Backcountry Lodge." Couple from California.

"I cannot say it enough, your staff is the best — warm, friendly, helpful. I didn't feel like a guest, I felt like family." Couple from Wisconsin.

Denali Wilderness Lodge

Contact: Bill McKinney
Address: PO Box 120
Trout Lake WA 98650
Phone: 509-395-2711
800-541-9779
Email: info@denaliwildernesslodge.com
Web: www.denaliwildernesslodge.com

A spectacular half-hour flight in an Alaskan bush plane brings you to the front door of Denali Wilderness Lodge. It began in 1907 as a hunting camp to provide fresh meat for gold miners and builders of the Alaska Railroad, and later, became an exclusive hunting lodge. Today, the only shooting you will see is with your camera. There are two dozen buildings, handcrafted from local spruce timber which was dragged to the site by horses and dog sleds.

You can stay in Cheechako Hotel, with six guestrooms and a central living room with wood stove, or choose one of four cabins set around the homestead, or one of six pairs of back-to-back cabins among alder and spruce trees down a winding path. The cabins are modern and comfortable with private baths.

Delicious meals are prepared daily and served in the main lodge, a two-story log building.

You can take guided and independent hikes in the Wood River Valley and surrounding slopes and ridges. Other hikes take you to the summit of Mount Anderson to see superb views of Mount McKinley and the Alaska Range. Horseback riding into the tundra-topped foothills or up to the ridge tops is also offered. If you stay for two or three nights, a 2½ hour ride is included. With four nights, you have two rides.

Expert naturalists will help you understand the wildlife which includes caribou, moose, Dall sheep, fox, wolf, and bear as well as many birds and other animals that live in the region. You may see wildflowers that carpet the ground in June and abundant wild blueberries in August.

In the evenings, there are campfires, after-dinner walks under the midnight sun, and wildlife films and interpretive programs. Later in the year, look for the magnificent show of the Northern Lights.

What you get: Accommodations, all meals, guided hiking, wrangler-guided horseback riding, interpretive and evening programs, gold panning. Air taxi and taxes not included.

What it costs:
$280 per person per night, quad room
$330 per person per night, double room
$430 per person per night, single room

"Bird songs for a wake-up call. Meadows of rainbow-hued wild-flowers. And a horseback ride above timberline for a better view. Ah wilderness — I'll take mine Denali Wilderness Lodge style." Visitor from Colorado.

Denver Museum of Nature and Science

Contact: Barbara Farley, Travel Programs
Address: 2001 Colorado Boulevard
Denver CO 80205-5798
Phone: 303-370-6304 Domestic travel
800-753-8272 Foreign travel
Fax: 303-370-8384
Email: bfarley@dmns.org
Web: www/dmns.org/domtrav.htm
www.dmns.org/inttours.htm

The renamed Museum — it used to be the Denver Museum of Natural History — provides adults and families with dozens of opportunities to travel and learn about nature and cultures with DMNS curators and educators

Dinosaur lovers can follow in the footsteps of gigantic Jurassic dinosaurs on a river-running expedition down the Green River in Utah and look for fossils, discover Indian rock art sites, and enjoy wilderness and wildlife. The trip includes a visit to Dinosaur National Monument to see a fossil bone quarry and models of life-size dinosaurs.

Explore Big Bend National Park, Texas, and admire the rugged Chisos Mountains, views of rolling hills and deserts, and vistas of wildflowers in bloom while you learn about the history of Apache and Comanche Indians, Buffalo Soldiers, cowboys, miners, and Mexicans who once lived there. There are also trips to the National Parks of the West by train, a tour of British Columbia, and a visit to Southeast Alaska.

Abroad, there is a trip to Egypt to discover the world of ancient pharoahs by visiting the pyramids of Giza, ancient Thebes, Abu Simbel, and the Valley of Kings. A ride down the Amazon River with DMNS zoology curator Cheri Jones will show you river dolphins, monkeys, sloths, and capybaras or guinea-pigs, as well as dozens of colorful birds. A two-week trip to South Africa will include the excitement of viewing the 2001 total solar eclipse. There is also a tour of Australia's lush coastal forests and empty stretches of untouched Outback.

You have to become a member of the Museum to participate in the tours; the annual fee is $35 for individuals, $65 for families, and $30 for seniors.

What you get: Accommodations, meals, transportation, DMNS study leaders, guides, entrance fees, pre-trip materials, reading lists.

What it costs:
$750 per adult, $600 per child 6 to 11, for 4 days, Vernal, Utah
$2,295 per adult for 7 days, Last Frontiers of Texas
$3,500 per adult for 9 days, Amazon River in Peru and Brazil.
$6,000 for 14 days, South Africa Solar Eclipse.

Dillman's Creative Art Workshops

Contact: Sue Robertson
Address: PO Box 98
            Lac du Flambeau WI 54538
Phone: 715-588-3143
Fax: 715-588-3110
Email: dillmans@newnorth.net
Web: www.dillmans.com

The Dillmans started Dillman's Sand Lake Lodge in 1935 planning to run a boys' camp. But when no boys showed up and families came to stay in the cabins, they gave up the idea and instead created a summer camp for families. Today, Dillman's is a popular and successful family-run vacations resort; in 1990, it was voted Best Cabin Resort in the country by readers of *Family Circle* magazine.

The lodge and cabins are set on a 15-acre peninsula in northern Wisconsin and are surrounded by acres of woodlands. There's swimming from two sandy beaches, a marina, a golf practice fairway, tennis courts, hiking and biking trails through the woods, nature walks, and the peaceful serenity of pristine 1,200-acre White Sand Lake. Karen

Caldwell and Doni Anderson provide excellent meals in the lakeside dining-room of Dillman's Lodge.

The Dillman's Creative Arts Foundation is now in its 24th season and brings nationally known artist instructors and holds special interest programs as part of the summer camp. Classes are offered from May to October in fully equipped classrooms overlooking the peaceful lake. Nationally known artists return year after year to teach week-long classes that cover a wide range of subjects including Bringing Landscapes to Life in Watercolor, Garden and Landscape Painting, Oil or Pastel Portraits and Landscape Painting, Gem Carving, Experimental Watermedia, Acrylic Wildlife Art, Painting with Mixed Media, Big Brush Watercolor, a photography camp, and a weekend wine tasting course.

As an extension of the art classes, artist Tom Lynch also offers a tour of England visiting Kew Gardens, London, Stratford, and the Cotswolds with the focus on sketchbook and water color paintings.

What you get: Accommodations Sunday through Friday night, instruction and 24-hour studio time Monday through Friday, model fees where applicable. Meals: all breakfasts, reception dinner Monday evening, cook-out Tuesday evening, dinner Thursday evening, mid-day Friday Champagne Celebration.

What it costs:
$795 for seven days, Artful Photography.
$875 for seven days, Watercolor by Design.
$985 for seven days, Gem Carving Bas Relief & Intaglio.
Scholarships are available. Day students accepted at lower fees.

Dude Ranchers' Association

Contact: Bobbi & Jim Futterer, Executive Directors
Address: PO Box 471-G
          LaPorte, CO 80535
Phone: 970-223-8440
Fax: 970-223-0201
Email: duderanches@compuserve.com
Web: www.duderanch.org

Learn how to be a cowboy at ranches in Arizona, Arkansas, California, Colorado, Idaho, Montana, Nevada, New Mexico, Oregon, South Dakota, Utah, and Wyoming where the real American West still survives. More than a hundred of these mostly family-owned ranches are members of the Dude Ranchers' Association, founded in 1926, which provides a rigorous inspection every two years for those ranches selected for membership.

A ranch vacation is an ideal way for families to get together. People of all ages come to find the easy-going relaxed Western lifestyle and to enjoy the wide range of activities available. You don't have to do anything — visitors can choose to ride a gentle horse on mountain pathways, hike along shady trails, swim in the pool or a river, fish in trout streams, soak in a hot tub, or sit in the porch rocking chair and admire the view. There are usually special programs for children that may include day care, active programs for youngsters of different ages, and events in the evening for teenagers.

The Association's web site is linked to the home pages of most of the ranches for more specific information about individual ranches which range from working cattle ranches, where "city slickers" can join cattle round-ups, to more luxurious ranch resorts, with hot tubs and gourmet food. All still preserve the flavor of the Western ranch with horseback riding, cookouts, hay rides, and other outdoor activities. Many offer swimming, fishing, hiking and wildlife viewing, as well as overnight pack trips and visits to nearby national parks. Year-round ranches may offer skiing, snow-boarding, snow-shoeing, and sledding in the winter.

The free annual directory gives detailed information with name, address, phone, email, web, when open, what's available, elevation, nearest airport, prices, and maps.

What you get: Accommodations, all meals, activities, horseback riding, ranch activities, equipment, instruction. Special diets available.

What it costs:
$900 to $2,400 per person for 7 days, depending on the ranch. Special prices for children.

On the following pages is a selection of ranches with different vacation styles.

Arizona
PRICE CANYON RANCH

Address: PO Box 1065
Douglas AZ 85608.
Phone: 800-727-0065
Email: pcranch@vtc.net
Web: www.pricecanyon.org

You can "giddyap!" with the real cowboys as you take part in an authentic roundup or join a spectacular trail ride to the top of the Chiricahua Mountains. Established in 1879, the Price Canyon Ranch is secluded in a majestic box canyon with golden grassy meadows and surrounded by the live oaks and ponderosa pines of Coronado National Forest. Year-round.

Colorado
C LAZY U RANCH

Address: PO Box 379
Granby CO 80446.
Phone: 970-887-3344
Email: ranch@clazyu.com
Web: www.clazyu.com

A luxury guest ranch, it's the only one to win both the Mobil Five Star and AAA Five Diamond ratings. There's an outdoor heated swimming pool, tennis, trap range, and fishing in a stream that flows through the property. The riding program, geared to all abilities, lets you ride the ridges, valleys, and meadows on a horse that's yours for the week. Year-round.

Idaho
TWIN PEAKS RANCH

Address: PO Box 774
Salmon ID 83467
Phone: 800-659-4899
Email: tpranch@earthlink.net
Web: www. Ranchweb.com/twinpeaks

Mountains, rivers, and lakes surround this 2,900-acre working ranch. There's a heated pool and hot tub. Other activities include a cattle roundup, trap shooting, fishing, a wilderness overnight tent camp in an elk preserve, a river camp with white-water rafting. Social time in the evenings includes line dancing, guitar sing-alongs, and a western band. June to October.

Montana
ELKHORN RANCH
Address: 33133 Gallatin Road
Gallatin Getaway MT 59730
Phone: 406-995-4291
Web: www.elkhornranchmt.com

Located at the northwest corner of Yellowstone National Park, the Elkhorn has been a family oriented ranch with horseback riding as the main activity since 1922. Individual log cabins, meals in the central dining room, a children's program where riding begins at six years old, and fly fishing in the nearby rivers. June to September.

Wyoming
PARADISE GUEST RANCH
Address: PO Box 790
Buffalo WY 82834
Phone: 307-684-7876
Email: fun@paradiseranch.com
Web: www.paradiseranch.com

Established in the scenic Big Horn Mountains of Wyoming in 1907, the ranch has luxury log cabins with fireplaces, outdoor decks, and spacious living rooms. There's also a heated pool, spa, and gourmet meals. Plenty of horseback riding, a fly fishing program with instruction, historical excursions, and complete children's programs. May to September.

Echo: The Wilderness Company

Contact: Joe Daly
Address: 6259 Telegraph Avenue
Oakland CA 94609
Phone: 510-652-1600
800-652-3246
Email: echo@echotrips.com
Web: www.echotrips.com

Echo was founded in 1971 by Joe Daly and Dick Linford and offers rafting trips on the Salmon River in Idaho, Tuolumne in California, and Rogue River in Oregon.

Each river has its own character. The Middle Fork of the Salmon in Idaho is America's premier alpine white-water river, and is listed as a protected Wild and Scenic River. The Main Salmon river, called The River of No Return by the National Geographic party that floated it in 1935, may offer glimpses of wildlife such as bighorn sheep, deer, or even a bear, a moose, or an eagle flying overhead. The Tuolumne is one of the most challenging rivers with big rapids, while the Rogue River is quieter with water warm enough for swimming.

Sometimes there's an educational emphasis like the Wine and Whitewater trip in June with an expert wine taster who explains the subtle nuances of both river and wine. Other special trips include the Bluegrass on Whitewater when musicians provide entertainment along the way, a fly fishing trip on the Salmon River to discover fantastic trout, and a Hiking/Rafting trip where you can hike along segments of the river trail.

For anyone who doesn't want to camp under the stars, there's a Lodge Trip where you spend nights at rustic riverside lodges. There are also river trips for kids led by Lori List who introduces them to the natural world, and family fun trips for families with children under 17.

What you get: Accommodations, most meals, transportation, guides, equipment, pre-trip material, reading lists, entertainment. Special diets available.

What it costs:
$369 per adult, 2 days, Tuolomne.
$500 per adult, 3 days, Rogue.
$1,070 per adult, 4 days, Lodge Trip, Main Salmon
$1,495 per adult, 6 days, Middle Fork Salmon.

"No other family vacation comes close to our incredible experience together on the Middle Fork." Family from California.

"One of the best weeks of my life, filled with never ending adventures and smiles." Participant from New York.

Eldertreks

Contact: Information
Address: Ellicott Station PO Box 11
Buffalo NY 14205-0011
Phone: 800-741-7956
Fax: 416-588-9839
Email: Info@eldertreks.com
Web: www.eldertreks.com

Designed for adventure travelers of 50 and over, Eldertreks offers hiking and other active trips to dozens of exotic locations including Cuba, Morocco, Kenya, Tibet, Hungary, Turkey, India, Borneo, Vietnam, Brazil, Costa Rica, Iceland, Finland, and New Zealand.

On a trip to Mongolia, participants join the celebrations for the Naadam Festival of horse riding, wrestling, and archery, travel to the rugged Alatai Mountains and visit Lake Hovsgol, and see Genghis Khan's legendary capital of Karkoram.

In Bolivia, there's a home stay on Taquile Island on Lake Titicaca. In Peru, there's a hike through the ancient ruins of Machu Picchu as well as boat trip up the Tambopata River in the Amazon Basin.

An Alaska cruise on a 10-passenger boat explores the fjords and inlets of the Alaskan Panhandle to see humpback and orca whales surface, watch glaciers break and fall into the ocean, and look for grizzly bears, bald eagles, sea lions, and mountain goats.

"A large part of our success as a company is due to our positive involvement in the communities we visit," notes a staff member. "We have been supporting hospitals, orphanages, schools, and environmental projects throughout the world with supplies and cash donations."

What you get: Accommodations, all meals, transportation, excursions, guides, instruction, pre-trip materials.

What it costs:
$2,995 for 15 days, Hungary & Romania
$3,295 for 19 days, Peru & Bolivia
$3,395 for 10 days, yacht cruise in Alaska

Esprit Travel

Contact: Steve Beimel
Address: 2101 Wilshire Boulevard
Santa Monica CA 90403
Phone: 310-829-6060
800-377-7481
Fax: 310-828-3564
Email: info@esprittravel.com
Web: www. esprittravel.com

Walking tours of Japan use radio technology so that tour leaders speak into a lapel microphone and participants listen to their guide through radio earphones. This is the hallmark of this company founded by Steve Beimel.

"Esprit tours are not for observers, they're for people who participate," he comments. "Rather than sitting on a bus, participants meet and experience the people of Japan up-close and personal."

On a walking tour you explore Kyoto, the jewel of Japanese culture. You see the quiet, charming residential neighborhoods and spend time with people who make their homes in Kyoto, visit some of the finest Japanese gardens, travel to a tiny 1,100-year-old nunnery in the mountains, and have a private tea ceremony with a Zen priest.

On a walking tour of northern Japan, you explore the rural Tohuku region hundreds of miles from bustling Tokyo. You watch farmers' wives in traditional costume pick vegetables, see orange persimmons on trees, admire apple orchards and vineyards, and stay at hot springs inns. A hike in the Japanese Alps reveals the lush natural greenery and the wilder mountain areas of Japan. You experience delicious local cuisine and soothing hot spring baths.

Other tours focus on music and theater, "taiko" drumming and traditional folk music, quilting and textiles in Kamakura and Kyoto, and Japanese gardens in Kyoto led by the publishers of the *Journal of Japanese Gardening.*

All walking tours use local trains or buses. Leaders are fluent in the language and long-time residents of Japan. Personal walking tours to meet special interests can be arranged. In addition, two-week trips in China and in Nepal are offered.

What you get: Airfare round trip from Los Angeles, accommodations, transportation, all breakfasts, most dinners, guides, touring, entrance fees, equipment, pre-trip material.

What it costs:
$3,150 for 12 days, Kyoto Original Walking Tour
$3,400 for 12 days, Rural Tour of Northern Japan
$4,000 for 12 days, Day Hikers Tour of the Japanese Alps

Experience Plus!

Contact: Rick & Paola Price
Address: 415 Mason Court, #1
               Fort Collins CO 80524
Phone: 970-484-8489
               800-685-4565
Fax: 970-493-0377
Email: tours@experienceplus.com
Web: www.experienceplus.com

Rick and Paola, who was born in Italy, met in Oregon. In 1972 they created bicycle tours of Italy as a way of returning to Italy every summer. Today they offer an ever-growing variety of biking and walking trips in beautiful parts of Italy, as well as in Greece, Spain, France, Switzerland, Denmark, Ireland, Costa Rica, New Zealand, the United States, and Canada throughout the year.

Though the Prices no longer lead every tour, they have selected expert bilingual guides, provide quality bicycles and full van support, choose small, local family inns with a private bathroom, for overnight stays, and pick places to eat where there's great food.

Cycling in Provence in the south of France begins in Aix-en-Provence, the birthplace of Paul Cezanne. From there you bike to the castle where Picasso lived in his later years and is buried, and on to Van Gogh country where so many of his best-known works were completed.

Walking in Italy through Tuscany shows you some of the most beautiful landscapes including the city of Florence with its churches and statues, and San Gimignano, a village with medieval towers and cobblestone streets.

One of the most popular trips is a bicycle ride across Italy from Pisa to Venice. The trip includes a stop in Vinci, where Leonardo da Vinci, was born to see scale models of his inventions in the local museum. There's an uphill climb over the Appenines through the Passo la Colla, and on to Faenza, followed by a visit to the farm which has been in Paola's family for more than a century, and then a ride through the Po Delta to Mesola, near the Adriatic.

What you get: Accommodations, most meals, wine with dinner on some tours, bicycle, support van, route map, bilingual escorts, traveling tour library, pre-trip material, pre-and-post-trip planning, all tips and gratuities, daily mileage options, special group events, water bottle, and choice of jersey, tee-shirt or fanny-pack.

What it costs:
$1,895 for 8 days, Walking the Oregon Coast.
$2,250 for 10 days, Cycling the Emerald Isle, Ireland.
$2,595 for 11 days, Cycling the Dordogne, France.
$3,295 for 15 days, Heart of Italy Walking.

"I really appreciated the way we were routed down back roads and through small villages. I felt we saw places we never could have found on our own." Couple from Oregon on Provence, France walking tour.

"If you are lucky enough to have lived in Paris as a young man, then wherever you go for the rest of your life, it stays with you. Paris is a movable feast." Ernest Hemingway

French-American Exchange

Contact: James Pondolfino
Address: 3213 Duke Street, #620
Alexandria VA 22314
Phone: 703-751-1586
800-995-5087
Fax: 703-823-4447
Email: faetours@erols.com
Web: www.faetours.com

Learn French while discovering the chateaux of the Loire River Valley, the museums of Paris, the secrets of Provence, or the sandy beaches of the Mediterranean.

Since 1987, the French-American Exchange has been offering language programs designed for independent travelers who share a passion for the French culture. You choose your location in Tours, Aix-en-Provence, Montpellier, Paris, or Nice. There are programs for college students, adults and seniors. Programs run year round and last from two weeks to an academic year. New this year are programs for children and teenagers on the French Riviera in Nice, Antibes, Aix, and Cannes which can be combined with adult programs for family summer vacations.

French language instruction is given mornings Monday through Friday for three to four hours in small groups. The curriculum includes oral and written communication, French civilization and culture, phonetics, pronunciation, and selected readings from classic and contemporary French literature and there are language labs, computer centers, and mediatech facilities.

In the afternoons there are workshops for adults on French poetry, music, art history, journalism, cuisine, cinema, translation and business French, while for youngsters there are sports, activities and excursions to places of interest, as well as evening programs.

Accommodations include home stays with a host family, student housing, renting furnished rooms in a private home, hotel, apartment, or a bed and breakfast.

What you get: Accommodations, most meals, tuition, fees, excursions.

What it costs:
$695 for 7 days, Summer Junior Programs
$859 for 14 days, Language Learning Vacations
$1,800 for 28 days, University Summer Program
$5,765 a semester, University Study Abroad

"This was the best learning vacation to take. The classes were challenging and intense. On tours, our phenomenal leader spoke to us in French about the destination and once there we could explore on our own. Everything exceeded my expectations." Woman at Aix-en-Provence summer program.

Friends of Fiber Art International

Contact: Camille J. Cook, President
Address: Box 468-TL
Western Springs IL 60558
Phone: 708-246-9466

Weavings, tapestries, silk paintings, quilts, baskets, embroidery, rugs, and related arts are the focus of this organization. On travel-and-learn tours, members attend important contemporary fiber art exhibitions here and in Europe, visit art museums and private collections. "Fiber arts" defines fine art made in flexible materials or works constructed using textile techniques; tapestry was its original form.

"Throughout history, fiber has been a rich and honored medium," notes a director of the organization which began in 1991. It now has more than 800 Friends in 46 states in the U.S. and 17 countries abroad.

A group of collectors, artists, and enthusiasts started the organization to increase appreciation and understanding of contemporary art in fiber media. The Friends have awarded more than $100,000 to encourage scholarship and critical writing about contemporary fiber art and supported traveling shows. Members can visit private collections and travel on group trips. Previous trips have been to the Lausanne Biennial in Switzerland and the Triennial in Lodz, Poland, both major exhibitions. Future plans include important fiber exhibitions in Belgium and Hungary, plus exciting weekends in many parts of America.

The Friends believe that the best way to help fiber artists is to develop a constituency of collectors to purchase their works. All surplus funds support projects that encourage collecting.

What you get: Accommodations, most meals, land transportation, entry fees, excursion, guides, pre-trip material. Participants make a $250 contribution to the organization.

What it costs:
$4,000 for 10 days in Poland, Spring 2001

"The schedule was intense, with five or six art events per day. The intellectual level of our companions was a plus. The trip was super." Participant on Poland tour.

"We kept seeing highlight after highlight. I've never seen so much great talent in so short a time. The incredible promise we saw in the student exhibition in Poland makes me lust to return to see how these youngsters develop." Participant on Poland tour.

Glickman-Popkin Bassoon Camp

Contact: Mark A. Popkin
Address: 740 Arbor Road
Winston-Salem NC 27104-2210
Phone: 336-725-5681
Fax: 336-777-8254
Email: elsiepop@aol.com

Want to brush up your bassoon playing at Master Classes in performance practices, reed making, and repertoire? Every summer professional bassoonists Loren Glickman and Mark Popkin offer a summer camp for experienced musicians over age 18, at Wildacres, a mountaintop retreat of 1,400 acres near Little Switzerland in the Blue Ridge Mountains. About a hundred bassoonists of all ages and stages come together to study, practice, and perform, and there are always guest artists who are principals in symphony orchestras or bassoon soloists. Mark Popkin also offers a one-week session on North Carolina's Emerald Isle.

Students attend lectures, practice, rehearse, and perform as soloists and in ensembles. Daily master classes by Loren Glickman and Mark Popkin are offered to advanced and intermediate students. Visiting guest musicians, bassoon repair and restoration experts, a bassoon manufacturing company representative, and an ever-ready accompanist also attend.

Mark Popkin has performed with the New York City Center Opera and Ballet, the New Jersey and Houston Symphony Orchestras, the Casals Festival, and the Mostly Mozart Festival, among others. Loren Glickman has performed as a soloist with the Chamber Music Society of Lincoln Center and the Casals Festival. He is currently on the faculties of Queens College, City University of New York, and the Juilliard School of Music.

What you get: Accommodations, all meals, instruction. A few part-scholarships are available.

What it costs:
$575 for 10 days, Glickman-Popkin Bassoon Camp
$475 for 10 days for non-bassoon-playing guests
$450 for 8 days, Mark Popkin's Camp

Global Volunteers

Contact: Volunteer Coordinator
Address: 375 E. Little Canada Road
St. Paul MN 55117-1628
Phone: 800-487-1074
Fax: 651-482-0915
Email: email@globalvolunteers.com
Web: www.globalvolunteers.org

Take a new kind of vacation, Service Learning Travel, to learn about a foreign culture by volunteering your time. Global Volunteers, which began in 1984, is a private non-profit group in Minnesota, offering dozens of ways you can volunteer by spending a few weeks in one of 18 countries or the U.S. working on specific projects. Last year, more than 150 volunteer teams worked with local people in communities around the world.

In Tanzania, teams laid down the wiring to provide electricity to the Mtera Secondary School and will help install a much-needed water pump and holding pump in this isolated village. In Poland, over the past ten years, volunteers have given English-language tutoring as part of a summer camp in the Tatra Mountains. In Romania, teams of volunteers provide cuddling and one-on-one care for toddlers at a failure-to-thrive clinic. In Ghana, volunteers helped build a wooden structure for a new pre-school.

The work projects are determined by the host communities and directed by local leaders. Participants experience immersion in the local community and its language, culture and traditions, as well as a first-hand experience of local living conditions and daily activities.

The program fees are tax-deductible and include a donation to the local community. The organization is in special consultative status in the United Nations.

What you get: Accommodations, all meals, team leader, tips, orientation, pre-trip material.

What it costs:
$450 for 7 days, any U.S. project
$1,895 for 14 days, Ecuador.
$1,995 for 14 days, Vietnam.

Volunteers and local women form a brick brigade, Pommern, Tanzania

Heartwood Home Building

Contact: Will Beemer
Address: Johnson Hill Road
Washington MA 01223
Phone: 413-623-6677
Fax: 413-623-0277
Web: www.heartwoodschool.com

Want to build your own house? Will and Michele Beemer of the Heartwood School in the Berkshire Hills can show you how.

"Heartwood was established in 1978 to teach the skills and knowledge it takes to build an energy-efficient house," Beemer explains. "The determination to become an active creator of your environment claims back your right to make a difference."

The school's approach is that "the best way to learn something is to *do* it," so students spend time in the classroom studying house mock-ups and models and then go and work at what they've learned: framing wall sections, calculating beam sizes, laying out a house foundation, orienting for solar exposure, and more. The three-week course covers all basic information and stresses energy efficiency and healthy, sustainable building techniques. The staff are licensed building contractors, and in addition there are carpenters, a mason, stone carver, and a timber frame construction expert. Sam Clark's *Designing and Building Your Own House Your Own Way* is the course text.

You can also take one-week courses on site planning and landscape design, renovation, cabinetmaking, timber framing, and carpentry for women, and weekend courses on bricklaying, tile, building with concrete blocks, and fireplace construction.

Usually about 15 people attend the house-building course and students have included teachers, truck drivers, architects, social workers, retirees, and high school students. The programs are geared to both skilled builders and beginners. Students provide their own tools.

What you get: Tuition and lunches. A list of local housing options is provided.

What it costs:
$500 per person for one week; $900 per couple for one week.
$1,250 per person for 3 weeks; $2,200 per couple for 3 weeks.

"The accepting, patient attitude on the part of the staff, who were very knowledgeable about construction and cared to teach the students to do good work. The experience has definitely enhanced my feeling of self-sufficiency." A social worker from New York.

HistoryAmerica Tours

Contact: Pete & Julia Brown
Address: PO Box 797687
            Dallas TX 75379
Phone: 972-713-7171
            800-628-8542
Fax: 972-713-7173
Web: www.historyamerica.com

This company offers 18 tours led by expert historians to fascinating places in American history. It also has a partnership with The History Channel and the Civil War Preservation Trust.

"We work closely with our Historian Guides, the experts in their fields, to plan itineraries that will offer the most valuable in-depth history experience anywhere," says director Pete Brown. "We've had travelers from all over the place: authors, Ph.Ds, photographers, cynics, Confederates, Yankees, antique hunters, bird watchers, and more."

The Red River Civil War Cruise takes participants on a river boat up the Mississippi to the Red River to visit the places affected by the 1864 campaign in Louisiana. The Union was preparing attacks on both Atlanta and Mobile when Union General Nathaniel Banks attempted to drive up the

Red River in Louisiana where he was soundly beaten. The tour's renowned guide is Ed Bearss, chief historian emeritus for the National Park Service.

The Civil War in the East explores Virginia's Shenandoah Valley where Philip Sheridan, a commander picked by Ulysses Grant to stop-attacks in the region, waged one of the most brilliant and decisive campaigns in American military history. Historian Guide Craig Howell leads the tour.

Another tour explores the short and violent life of Billy the Kid. You travel to New Mexico and White Oaks, where Billy disposed of his stolen cattle and horses, the Hubbard Museum of the American West in Ruidoso, Fort Sumner State Park, and Billy's grave, and have dinner with a historian in Albuquerque.

Participants stay in comfortable hotels or aboard cruise ships.

What you get: Accommodations, transportation, entry fees, taxes, historian guides, instruction, films, pre-trip material, reading lists, most meals, guest appearances by well-known historians.

What it costs:
$1,495 per person, double, for 8 days, The Apache Wars
$1,795 per person, double, for 9 days, Historic Texas
$2,060 to $4,790 per person, double, for 9 days, Red River Civil War Cruise.

"Neil Mangum is a perfect 10. He brought the Apaches to life for me. He is a gifted historian. All in all it was a truly memorable experience." Woman from Pennsylvania on Apache Wars tour.

"I could not ask for more. Taking a tour with HistoryAmerica is much more enjoyable and educational than taking college level history classes." Man from Indiana with Dakota Legacy.

Idyllwild Arts

Contact: Heather Companiott
Address: PO Box 38
Idyllwild CA 92549
Phone: 909-659-2171
Fax: 909-659-5463
Email: heatherc@idyllwildarts.org
Web: www.idyllwildarts.org

Idyllwild Arts, established in 1950 as an arts education center, offers a wide range of summer courses in the arts for students of all ages through its Children's Center, Junior Artists Center, Youth Arts Center, and Adult Center.

The dozens of classes include dance, vocal music, jazz workshop, orchestral music, choral singing, piano workshop, landscape painting, self-publishing with computers, poetry, creative writing, ceramics, printmaking, collage, life drawing, photography, mixed media, and watercolor workshops. There's also a unique series of Native American visual arts taught by Navajo, Hopi and Zuni experts in jewelry making, weaving, silversmithing, pottery, coiled baskets, and flute making.

Special programs include Distinguished Artists Residencies that bring artists to the campus. A Summer Poetry program celebrates poetry with nightly readings by poets and daily lectures and discussions. An Art, Archaeology, and History week studies Native American Arts and Culture of California and the Southwest with seminars and a dance festival. Future topics will look at chamber music and contemporary painting.

Idyllwild is located on the western slopes of the San Jacinto Mountains in Southern California, at 5,000 feet above sea level. The 205-acre campus is beautifully set amid alpine forests and mountain meadows and has artists studios, indoor and outdoor theaters, dance studios, piano practice rooms, comfortable lodgings and a main dining room.

Families enjoy the week-long Family Camp in July with outdoor activities and art programs.

What you get: Instructors, workshops, equipment, instructions. Accommodations in dorm rooms or nearby motels or cabins must be booked separately.

What it costs:
$325 for 3 days, Intensive Poetry Writing
$440 for 6 days, Small Scale Bronze Casting
$1,195 for 7 days, Family Camp, two people in a room

"In addition to working in silver, I learned something about myself and about the philosophy and attitudes of a different and remarkable culture." Student in Native American Arts program.

International Bicycle Fund

Contact: David Mozer
Address: 4887-H Columbia Drive South
Seattle WA 98108-1919
Phone: 206-767-0848
Fax: 206-767-0848
Email: ibike@ibike.org
Web: www.ibike.org/ibike

IBF is a non-profit organization that assists economic development by encouraging the use of bicycles. It also sponsors educational bicycle travel programs to Ecuador, Cuba, Nepal, Tunisia, Zimbabwe, and across East and West Africa.

"It's a people-to-people program for all good-natured realists who appreciate the rewards of self-contained bicycle touring, the diversity in the world, and the chance to remove the barriers between you, the land and its people," notes David Mozer, an Africa studies specialist and pioneer of bicycle touring in Africa and responsible travel.

In Tunisia, participants can expect to cycle about 40 miles a day on paved roads. They meet rural villagers, skilled craftsmen, educators, and officials, learn about the changing role of women, and visit desert oases and historic sites dating back to the second century. Overnights are spent in comfortable hotels.

In Mali, the group explores the historical rich grasslands area, visiting Djenne, the Dogon Country and fabled Timbuktu. In Uganda, the tour travels through the western region visiting development programs, tea estates, and national parks. Both tours includes some dirt roads.

All participants receive a comprehensive pre-departure book about bicycling in Africa, with detailed instructions on setting up bicycles and what to expect.

What you get: Accommodations, local airfare, most meals, transportation, transfers, instruction, entry fees, guides, excursions, reading lists, pre-trip material. Some special diets available.

What it costs:
$990 for 14 days, Cuba
$1,190 for 14 days, Tunisia
$1,490 for 14 days, Tanzania

"A month on a Bicycle Africa trip is worth four years of college anthropology courses. Thank you for the greatest experience of my life." Senior participant from California.

"The bicycle was vital to the experience. It gave us time to see and to reflect on what we were seeing. The very uniqueness of our mode of travel also served as an icebreaker whenever we met anyone." Participant from New York.

International Expeditions

Contact: Tour Information
Address: One Environs Parks
Helena AL 35080
Phone: 205-428-1700
800-633-4734
Fax: 205-428-1714
Email: nature@ietravel.com
Web: www.ietravel.com

Since 1981, International Expeditions has offered quality nature travel programs to create environmental awareness and conservation through travel. Its purpose is "to stimulate an interest in, develop an understanding of, and create an appreciation for the great natural wonders of our Earth."

Expert naturalist guides lead all the tours. Several trips explore the Amazon region where you visit the Amazon Center for Environmental Education and Research (ACEER) and the completed Canopy Walkway used by scientists and researchers in the rain forest. You can also take a voyage on a classical Amazon river boat from Lima in Peru down the river through some of the most exotic scenery in the world. Here you may see gray and pink river dolphins, giant water lilies, squirrel monkeys, and hundreds of species of birds unique to the region.

Other trips take you to look at the natural world in Belize, Costa Rica, the Galapagos Islands, Patagonia, Africa, Australia, Bali, Komodo, and Alaska.

The company also offers an Independent Nature Travel program for those who want to create their own itinerary. You can go on a safari to Africa and visit the places and animals you really long to see on a specially designed journey. Expert mountain guides can lead you to the top of Mount Kilimanjaro. Other trips visit Machu Picchu, the Urubamba River, and the Sacred Valley in Peru, or travel to Antarctica to cruise among ice floes, wander among nesting penguins, and observe whales and seals.

What you get: Airfare from gateway city, accommodations, transportation, excursions, most meals, naturalist guides, activities, pre-trip information.

What it costs:
$2,798 for 10 days, Costa Rica
$3,798 for 12 days, Brazil's Pantanal
$4,998 for 17 days, Tanzania and Kenya

"Going on your expedition to the Pantanal was an experience of a lifetime. Everyone would benefit from seeing such an extraordinary place." Man from Virginia on Brazil trip.

"The attention to detail was excellent. Our guides were well-educated and really wanted us to understand the islands and the eco-system." Woman from Delaware on Galapagos Islands trip.

James Henry River Journeys

Contact: James Katz
Address: PO Box 807
Bolinas CA 94924
Phone: 415-868-1836
800-786-1830
Fax: 415-868-9033
Email: jhrj@riverjourneys.com
Web: www.riverjourneys.com

For 28 years, this company has provided joyful in-depth wilderness experiences on North America's most spectacular and pristine rivers. Combining adventure with learning and camaraderie, trip participants are encouraged to take the less-traveled path and to immerse themselves in the exhilaration of whitewater and the joy of wilderness living. You can travel in a paddleboat, inflatable kayak, canoe, or oarboat.

Rivers have a unique character and personality. In Alaska, the Tatshenshini and Alsek Rivers flow through North America's most spectacular and pristine wilderness areas.

You can observe eagle, moose, mink, beaver, black and Alaskan brown bears.

On Oregon's Rogue, you travel through a lush canyon with challenging rapids and hike on an inspiring trail. The Klamath is a stunning river cutting through a precipitous range of mountains. There are warm-water rapids and a hike up a fern-lined side canyon replete with waterfalls.

Special Interest Trips are a hallmark of this company. In California and Oregon, you can join music trips that focus on Renaissance, baroque or classical music, and wine tasting with some of the region's most respected winemakers. In Alaska, special programs incorporate the themes of Native American tales, bear mythology, cultural anthropology, and natural history.

What you get: Accommodations, camping, transportation to and from meeting point, all meals, entry fees, guides, equipment, instruction, pre-departure material, reading lists. Prices vary for adults, youths, and groups.

What it costs:
$320 to $445 per person, 3-day Family Plan or Special Interest Trip, Klamath River
$535 to $825 for 4 to 5 days, Special Interest Trip, Rogue River, Oregon.
$2,675 for 11 days, Tatshenshini-Alsek, Alaska.

Journeys East

Contact: Davis Everett & Debra Loomis
Address: PO Box 1161
Middletown CA 95461
Phone: 707-987-4531
800-527-2612
Fax: 707-987-4831
Email: trips@journeyseast.com
Web: www.journeyseast.com

Specializing in vacations that show travelers how to immerse themselves in another culture, Journeys East offers trips to Japan, China and Scotland.

From Farmhouse to Teahouse explores Japan's folk architecture and regional cuisine. You start in Tokyo and go north to stay in thatched-roof farmhouses, traditional hot springs inns, and historic villages. You explore the temples of Nagano, the lacquerware of Kiso Valley, and the sake breweries of Takayama.

On Brushes with Inner Japan, you study traditional influences on contemporary design with visits to sculpture gardens, master artisans, receive instruction in Zen meditation and in flower arranging. There's also a moonlight dip in a waterfall at a Shinto shrine, hot springs bathing at a samurai's manor, and an island stay at a combined art museum and hotel.

A tour of China and Japan compares the roots and evolution of East Asian traditions. You visit Hong Kong to look at traditional brush painting and contemporary Chinese art, Hangzhou to learn about Taoism, Confucianism and Buddhism, Suzhou to see Ming gardens, silk weaving and literary sites, and end the journey in Kyoto to see Japanese interpretations of Chinese traditions.

In addition, the company now offers tours of Scotland's northwestern highlands and islands with hikes along the coast, visits to shepherds and historians, and whiskey tasting.

What you get: Accommodations, most meals, transportation, tips, guides, instruction, entry fees, pre-trip material, maps, reading lists.

What it costs:
$3,985 for 16 days, Highland Journey, Scotland
$4,485 for 15 days, From Farmhouse to Teahouse, Japan
$5,500 for 15 days, Tracing Traditions, China and Japan

"The more I traveled, the more I realized that fear makes strangers of people who should be friends."
Shirley MacLaine

Journeys International

Contact: Will & Joan Weber
Address: 107 Aprill Drive, Suite 3
Ann Arbor MI 48103-1903
Phone: 734-665-4407
800-255-8735
Fax: 734-665-2945
Email: info@journeys-intl.com
Web: www.journeys-into.com

This company promotes nature and culture conservation and also works with local communities to encourage ecology and preservation. Many of its guides are professionally employed in conservation or local development projects.

Founded in 1978, it offers hundreds of international adventure, cultural and nature-oriented explorations as well as custom arrangements for individual trips. In East Africa, there are active safaris to Kenya and Tanzania, where you can climb Mount Kilimanjaro, as well as tours to Namibia, Ethiopia, and Southern Africa. You can see Tanzania's wild animals, Uganda's primates, and the wildlife in Zimbabwe and Zambia. There are also trips to Morocco including a trek through the High Atlas mountains.

Other trips visit Central and South America with nature trips to Costa Rica and Belize, Panama, Brazil, Chile, Bolivia, Peru, and the Galapagos. In Europe you can travel in Italy, Greece, England, and Turkey. Asian trips take you to the Himalayas, Bhutan, Burma, China, India, Tibet, Laos, Cambodia, Thailand, and Vietnam. There are several expeditions in Nepal including an Everest Lodge Trek. You can also travel to Hawaii, Samoa, Indonesia, Australia, and New Zealand.

The company also offers special family trips that take you to a range of places including Greece, Panama, Belize, Peru, Nepal, Australia, Costa Rica, and Tanzania.

When it began, the company established the non-profit Earth Preservation Fund which helps local communities protect their natural and cultural heritage. Projects include distributing native seedlings for plantings, holding ecotourism workshops for local communities, teaching traditional weaving techniques that were being forgotten, helping set up a school to teach Tibetan culture, history, and religion, and providing funding for a hostel for young monks.

What you get: Accommodations, transportation, most meals, permits, equipment, guides, pre-trip material. Airfare not included, but group fares can be arranged.

What it costs:
$2,000 for 10 days, Hiking Odyssey, Hawaii
$2,095 for 16 days, Annapurna Family Trek, Nepal
$3,390 to $4,150 for 13 days, Tanzania Culture and Wildlife

"The entire trip wildly exceeded my expectations, which were already high!" Woman from Maryland on Galapagos trip.

Journeys Into American Indian Territory

Contact: Robert Vetter
Address: PO Box 575
         Eastport NY 11941
Phone: 631-878-8655
         800-458-2632
Fax: 516-878-4518
Email: info@indianjourneys.com
Web: www.indianjourneys.com

A unique opportunity to learn from modern American Indians on their own territory is offered by this company created in 1988 by anthropologist Robert Vetter, who studied at the University of Oklahoma. He realized that many people read about Native Americans but never have the chance to meet and talk with them or to experience their customs and traditions. He takes small groups for a total immersion experience in native American cultures.

The core program, featured on TV's Travel Channel, visits the Oklahoma southern plains to see where the Cheyenne, Arapahoe, Kiowa, Comanche, Apache, and Caddo peoples live today. You stay in a modern guest house or a traditional tipi, and go hiking and horseback riding. You learn traditional dances, visit a Kiowa family in their home, attend their clan pow-wow, and explore the Wichita Mountains, a center of spiritual and ceremonial importance to the Plains tribes.

In New York's Catskill Mountains there's a weekend of native cultures, music, dance, and traditions that brings together several tribes. The program is led by Moses Starr, a Southern Cheyenne elder, and Tom Porter, a Mohawk spiritual leader. Two other weekend programs take you to Kanatsiohareke, a Mohawk traditional community near Albany, New York, to learn Iroquois herbal and healing traditions, and also to study the teachings of the Peacemaker, spiritual principles, and the clan system.

The company also offers home stays with Native American families and special school programs.

What you get: Accommodations, transportation, most meals, entry fees, excursions, guides, instruction, reading lists, tips, pre-trip material.

What it costs:
$340 for 3 days, Mohawk Teachings, New York
$380 for 3 days, A Gathering of Peoples, Catskills, New York
$875 for 9 days, The Southern Plains Experience, Oklahoma.

"If you admire and respect Native Americans as I do, there is no lottery you can win to compare to what you will learn and experience on one of these journeys." Woman from California.

"I felt that Journeys provided me with a glimpse into another world, a world that I find superior to our current mainstream American reality." Man from New York.

Kosciuszko Foundation

Contact: Addy Tymczyszyn
Address: 15 East 65 Street
New York NY 10021-6595
Phone: 212-734-2130
Fax: 212-628-4552
Email: thekf@aol.com
Web: www.kosciuszkofoundation.org

The Foundation was created in 1925 to promote educational and cultural exchanges between the United States and Poland and to increase American understanding of Polish culture and history. It is named after Thaddeus Kosciuszko who enlisted in the American army during the Revolutionary War in 1775. As a national not-for-profit, nonpartisan, and nonsectarian organization, it awards one million dollars in grants and scholarships for education each year, with more than $490,000 to Americans of Polish descent for studies in the United States for the academic year 2001-2002.

Summer courses in Poland are offered at universities from June to August. They are open to graduates and undergraduates as well as to graduating high school students who are 18 and over, and non-traditional older students interested in the programs.

At Jagiellonian University in Krakow you can sign up for three, four, and six week sessions in either Art or a Polish language program. Seminars include Polish Art since the 14th century, Polish Film, the Jews of Poland, Polish Music, and more. Language instruction is offered at beginner, intermediate, and advanced levels. Most language classes demand five hours a day of intensive study, while others require only three hours a day of study.

The Polish Institute of Christian Culture has classes in Polish and English on the history, literature, art, society, and theater and film of Poland, and includes sightseeing trips to Rome and an audience with the Pope. The Catholic University of Lublin offers language classes at non-intensive, intensive, and highly intensive levels.

Students live in dorms, with shared toilet and bathing facilities, and take their meals in student dining halls. The Foundation warns participants to be prepared for a great deal of walking to classes and stair climbing, since there are no elevators.

What you get: Accommodations, all meals, tuition, excursions, cultural activities.

What it costs:
$815 for 14 days, Intensive Polish, Catholic University, Lublin
$1,220 for 28 days, Language & Arts, Jagiellonian University, Krakow
$1,270 for 28 days, Art class, Jagiellonian University, Krakow

Lindblad Expeditions

Contact: Sven-Olof Lindblad
Address: 720 Fifth Avenue
New York NY 10019
Phone: 212-765-7740
800-397-3348
Fax: 212-265-3370
Web: www.expeditions.com

Lindblad Expeditions offer adventure travel trips to dozens of destinations around the world, mostly aboard comfortable expedition ships carrying between 30 and 110 guests, and provide Zodiac boats for landings and kayaks for paddlers.

"While every expedition embraces a spirit of adventure, you always travel in comfort," notes director Sven-Olof Lindblad. "Naturalists and historians share their knowledge and expertise with you, and you enjoy tasteful accommodations, wholesome food, an attentive staff and a refreshingly informal atmosphere."

Visit Antarctica to see penguins and icebergs, including a special photography trip led by a professional photographer. In 1966, Sven-Olof Lindblad's father, Lars-Eric, pioneered the first travel expedition to Antarctica and spent almost every winter there until his death in 1994. He was honored by the United States Advisory Committee on Antarctic names in 1996 when an area of Antarctica's Charcot Bay was named Lindblad Cove after him.

The company, founded in 1979, today offers dozens of trips to explore such places as the Galapagos Islands off the coast of Ecuador to see giant tortoises, blue-footed boobies and land and sea iguanas. You can visit Baja California and spend two weeks floating in the Gulf of California, which Jacques Cousteau called "a marine aquarium with the greatest diversity of life on earth," to snorkel and kayak, see whales, and visit many of the small islands and remote bays of the Baja peninsula. You can also travel down the rivers of the west or visit Mexico's Copper Canyon, Costa Rica, Panama, Saudia Arabia, and Jordan.

What you get: Accommodations, all meals, transfers, excursions, snorkeling equipment and sea kayaks, tips, taxes, services charges, services of ship's physician, expert guides, pre-trip material, reading lists.

What it costs:
$2,790 to $4,890 for 8 days, double room, Costa Rica and Panama.
$3,700 to $5,900 for 14 days, double room, Baja California.
$9,600 to $16,800 for 18 days, double room, Antarctica and the Falklands.

"This was a fantastic trip with incredible landings. We loved the naturalists. This was the trip of a lifetime and very well done. We had very high expectations and were not disappointed." Couple from California on Antarctic trip.

Maine Windjammers Association

Contact: Information
Address: PO Box 1144
Blue Hill ME 04614
Phone: 800-807-9463
Email: windjam@acadia.net
Web: www.sailmainecoast.com

Want to sail in a 19th century windjammmer? You can spend a week on a refurbished schooner under the command of a U.S Coast Guard-licensed captain and explore the coast of Maine. You enjoy days at sea with the wind billowing out the huge sails and evenings moored in harbors and island coves, rocking on the ripples. You see seals, porpoises, whales, eagles, puffins, and osprey. You can go ashore every day, or stay aboard, swim, or row the skiff. You visit pristine islands and quaint Maine fishing villages.

Once aboard, you have a comfortable cabin with windows, a sink with fresh running water, and hot and cold showers. The meals are ample with fish chowder, hot biscuits, roast beef, fresh vegetables, and lobster cooked on the beach. You can learn to lower the mainsail, take the wheel, coil the lines, cat the anchor, splice ropes, and steer by the stars, or just relax on deck.

In the evening, anchored in a quiet harbor, dinner is served on deck, and, if the mood is right, the captain plays sailors' tunes on his old concertina or reads classic sea stories.

The Maine Windjammer Association represents 13 refurbished wind-powered boats, including the *American Eagle, Heritage, Isaac H. Evans, Mary Day,* and *Timberwind.* Each boat is unique and holds between 20 and 40 passengers. The *Nathaniel Bowditch,* built as a racing schooner in 1922, won a special class honors in the Bermuda Race in 1923 and served in the Coast Guard in World War II. The *Isaac H. Evans* was built in New Jersey, in 1886, and is now a National Historic Landmark. Completely rebuilt, there are 11 double-berth cabins, all with a window, reading light over the bunkbed, and a sink with running water. The *American Eagle,* a fishing boat for 53 years, was carefully restored using historical research to make sure everything was correct. The *Heritage* was designed along the lines of a 19th century coaster and launched in 1983.

What you get: Accommodations, meals, guides, instruction, excursions.

What it costs:
$309 to $795 for 3, 4, 5, or 6 day cruises along Maine coast. Prices vary according to month chosen, lengths of cruise and schooner.

"What a great trip! It's both relaxing and energizing. I have been asked whether it's the food or the sailing that we go for, and I have to admit that it's both." Couple from Illinois.

"We loved the sailing, birding, islands, the superb food, storytelling, and the terrific sense of humor aboard." Couple from Virginia.

"I must go down to the seas again,
 to the lonely sea and sky;
And all I ask is a tall ship,
and a star to steer her by."

John Masefield

Maine Windjammer Victory Chimes

Contact: Victory Chimes
Address: PO Box 1401
             Rockland ME 04841
Phone: 207-265-5651
             800-745-5651
Email: chimes@sunline.net
             kipfiles@aol.com
Web: www.victorychimes.com

All windjammers are unique - but *Victory Chimes* is significant because she is the largest passenger sailing vessel under the U.S. flag and the only three-masted schooner.

She was built at a Delaware shipyard in 1900 as a coastal freight-carrier named the *Edwin & Maude*. Made of the finest Georgia pine, live oak, and Delaware oak, she carried lumber up and down Chesapeake Bay for more than 50 years. She was converted to a cruise ship in 1945 and came to Maine in 1954.

Her captain, Richard "Kip"Files, grew up in Maine, and has been crewing on large traditional sailing craft since the early 1970s. He first saw the schooner when he was asked to oversee its restoration, and later, when it was offered for sale, he bought it with Captain Paul DeGaeta and the *Victory Chimes* sailed again.

On April 15, 2000, she celebrated her 100th anniversary with a gala celebration at the Chesapeake Bay Maritime Museum in Maryland and then sailed to Penobscot Bay, Maine. In June, *Boat International USA* named her one of the "top 200 yachts in the world." A fund has been launched to raise money to refurbish her so she can survive for another century.

The *Victory Chimes* holds 40 guests, has hot showers, push-button toilets, and space to walk around. On a cruise, you sail along the Maine coast under vast, billowing sails, and stop at Isle Au Haut, a spectacular island that is part of Acadia National Park, Somes Sound, which resembles a Norwegian fjord, Castine, the home of the Maine Maritime Academy, Boothbay Harbor, a picturesque Maine coastal village, and some of the outer islands such as Vinalhaven, Swans Island, and Monhegan, and lobster or fishing communities.

Says the captain: "Where we go is up to Mother Nature. I never know where I'll be taking the boat, but wherever we go, I guarantee you that it's going to be beautiful."

What you get: Accommodations, all meals, transportation, excursions, instruction, guides.

What it costs:
$550 to $800 for 4, 5 or 7 days, depending on cruise.

Mobility International and National Clearinghouse on Disability and Exchange

Contact: Coordinator
Address: PO Box 10767
Eugene OR 97440
Phone: 541-343-1284 (Voice or TTY)
Fax: 541-343-6812

During its 20-year history, exchanges to and from many countries of the world have been offered by this unique organization which encourages people with disabilities to travel with a purpose. The group provides free information and program referral services, publishes books, manuals and vidos, and offers a limited number of its own international leadership development exchanges.

MIUSA (Mobility International USA) is a national not-for-profit organization whose purpose is to promote international educational exchange and community service overseas for people with or without disabilities. Depending on funding, MIUSA sponsors youth leadership and professional exchange opportunities focused on disability issues and empowerment, and has held international leadership conferences in Oregon.

"Disabled people need to be part of the educational exchange experience," notes one traveler. "Participants in these programs need to learn to accept and respect differences not only of people in other cultures, but also of people with different abilities in their own country and throughout the world."

MIUSA recently produced a video, *All Abroad!*, funded by the U.S. Department of State, that highlights people with disabilities who describe their experiences overseas and answer frequently asked questions. The video is available with captions and audio descriptions.

What you get: *A World Awaits You,* annual journal, free. *Over the Rainbow,* bi-annual newsletter availble with membership ($30). *A World of Options: A Guide to International Exchange, Community Service and Travel for Persons with Disabilities* ($35). All Abroad! video, ($49).

What it costs:
$35 MIUSA membership for individuals
$50 for local or state organizations
$150 for national organizations

"Sure there are obstacles, but it's worth all the trouble." Exchange student who is a quadriplegic.

"I traveled and stayed with families all over Europe." Traveler who is blind.

Myths and Mountains

Contact: Antonia Neubauer, President
Address: 976 Tee Court
Incline Village, NV 89451
Phone: 775-832-5454
800-670-6984
Fax: 775-832-4454
Email: travel@mythsandmountains.com
Web: mythsandmountains.com

Specializing in nontraditional journeys off the beaten track, the company looks for travel that truly defines the country you visit. In Vietnam you learn about the French Colonial Heritage, in the Amazon you meet shamans, in Peru you study Inca rituals, and in India the Rajput heritage.

You can also take specialized tours for individuals in collaboration with regional operators designed to emphasize environmental, cultural, and historical themes so travelers learn firsthand about the people and their culture from local guides. Destinations include Nepal, Tibet, Bhutan, Chile, Costa Rica, and Ecuador.

You can spend Christmas in Nepal and stay in a Sherpa home high in the Himalaya, visit schools and clinics in villages, pray with monks, and explore the region's surrounding fields and streams on light trekking expeditions.

In Thailand and Laos, you visit tribal villages and cities to see the lifestyles of the Hmong, Lisu, Lahu, among other tribes. You learn their crafts, participate in their rituals, and eat their foods, and have time to explore the mountains and caves, bathe in waterfalls, and shop in local markets.

"We remain unique in offering learning journeys in an industry that still focuses on destinations," notes Dr. Antonio Neubauer. "For us, the dream is to make a journey."

The company makes a contribution to local places, has helped to build a library in Nepal, assisted the disabled in Thailand, and traveled with volunteer groups in Asia or South America.

What you get: Accommodations, transportation, most meals, excursions, guides, entry fees, equipment, reading lists.

What it costs:
$1,406 for 8 days, Amazon River cruise
$1,995 for 16 days, Christmas in Nepal
$2,395 for 18 days, Thai Massage & Hill Tribe Villages, Thailand

"For ten days, we explored life in Ecuador. The best part was Rio Blanco, where we were stripped of all technology and were able to escape the modern world and just revel in the beauty of nature and the culture of an indigenous society. It was amazing." Student from Emory University on Shamans of Ecuador trip.

National Audubon Society

Contact:	Margaret M. Carnright, Director Travel,
Address:	700 Broadway
	New York NY 10003
Phone:	212-979-3067
Fax:	212-979-8947
Email:	mcarnright@audubon.org
Web:	www.audubon.org/market/no/

Audubon Nature Odysseys are led by staff experts and focus on birds, plants, animals, wildlife sanctuaries, and nature refuges around the world. The Society has sponsored travel programs for its members since the 1940s.

The Society takes travelers on safaris around the world including Tanzania and Namibia, Botswana and Victoria Falls, Antarctica, Australia and New Zealand, Baja California, Cuba, Scandinavia, the Galapagos Islands, India, Nepal, and China.

In the US, trip destinations include Alaska, an exploration of the Intracoastal Waterway from Florida to South Carolina with tours of 19th century mansions and antebellum plantations. There are also tours of the National Parks of the West.

In 1989, concerns for the environment led the Society to prepare a statement, *The National Audubon Society Travel*

Ethic for Environmentally Responsible Travel, that provides clear requirements for tour operators, leaders, and participants, which is now available in English and Spanish. The key points stress:

1. Wildlife and their habitats must not be disturbed.
2. Audubon tourism to natural areas will be sustainable.
3. Waste disposal must have neither environmental nor aesthetic impact.
4. The experience a tourist gains in traveling with Audubon must enrich his or her appreciation of nature, conservation, and the environment.
5. Audubon tours must strengthen the conservation effort and enhance the natural integrity of places visited.
6. Traffic in products that threaten wildlife and plant populations must not occur.
7. The sensibilities of other cultures must be respected.

What you get: Accommodations, transportation, most meals, excursions, entrance fees, equipment, instruction, pre-trip material, reading lists, transfers, tips, taxes, service charges, ship physician, lectures, guides. Special diets available.

What it costs:

$2,235 to $3,900 for 10 days, Galapagos Islands, Ecuador

$6,695 for 12 days, Okavango Safari, Africa, includes airfare from New York

$7,690 to $13,590 for 16 days, New Zealand and its sub-Antarctic Islands

"The trip was fantastic, in no small part due to the naturalists on board. I look forward to traveling with them again." Participant from Illinois on Antarctica & Falkland Islands tour.

National Registration Center for Study Abroad

Contact: Ann Wittigor & Reuel Zielke
Address: PO Box 1393
Milwaukee WI 53201
Phone: 414-278-0631
Fax: 414-271-8884
Email: study@nrcsa.com
Web: www.nrcsa.com

The NRCSA, a consortium of more than 100 universities, foreign language institutes and adult education centers in 38 countries, has a motto: Live the Culture, Learn the Language.

In 1999, a survey of NRCSA members reported that more than 25,000 Americans traveled and studied with them, ranging in age from 17 to 84. One survey showed that in some regions there are more younger students in the summer and more mature adults the rest of the year. Homestay programs enable students to live and study at the home of their own private teacher in a language immersion program that is available in dozens of countries. Students can also take classes in cooking, art, literature, and music, or serve as volunteers and interns on trekking and adventure travel trips.

You find university students, mature adults, professionals, and people from all walks of life participating in NRCSA programs. Additionally, most school have diverse student groups with students from all over the world attending the same school. Teachers from more than 1,000 school districts have attended courses for graduate credits, in-service credit, and personal enrichment.

NRSCA offers programs for teenagers either in groups accompanied by a teacher or go on their own to structured teen programs abroad in such places as Mexico, Spain, Costa Rica and France.

Complete information is published in catalogs for studying a wide array of language programs year-round including Arabic, Chinese, Danish, Dutch, Finnish, Gaelic, Greek, Hebrew, Hungarian, Italian, Japanese, Latin, Mayan, Norwegian, Portuguese, and Swedish. Credit transfer is available through a network of universities.

What you get: Accommodations, meals, insurance, lectures, field trips. For information on program dates and fees, send a self-addressed business envelope with 55 cents postage.

What it costs:
$838 for 14 days, German and literature, Germany.
$959 for 14 days, Italian and opera, Italy.
$1,240 for 8 weeks, Spanish and volunteering, Peru.
$1,677 for 21 days, French and cooking, France.

"The learning experience was excellent. I am a Spanish teacher and it was invaluable practice. The family was fabulous, super friendly, kind, thoughtful, good food and atmosphere." A teacher from Boston.

National Trust for Historic Preservation

Contact: Director Travel Programs
Address: 1785 Massachusetts Avenue NW
Washington DC 20036
Phone: 202-588-6300
800-944-6847
Fax: 202-588-6246
Email: tours@nthp.org
Web: www.nthp.org

For more than 30 years, National Trust Study Tours have been offering superior programs to dozens of destinations to explore the traditions and cultures of the world with special emphasis on the effect that art and architecture has had on them. There are more than 85 distinct and diverse itineraries that provide exclusive access to significant private homes, collections, castles, and fascinating people, and tours are led by expert study leaders, local guides and a professional staff. You stay in superior lodgings in luxurious surroundings and enjoy sumptuous cuisine prepared by master chefs.

Among trips available is a program in Mandarin China that includes a week's cruise down the Yangtze River with special tours at stops not offered on most China tours. In England, you experience the beginning of the London Season from the Royal Enclosure at Ascot as well as explore London. You study native traditions and visit the kennels of Iditarod dogs in Alaska. A program in Colonial Bermuda explores the architectural styles and natural beauty of the island and includes visits to private homes and meetings with representatives of the Bermuda National Trust.

What you get: Airfare (on most international tours) transportation, accommodations, most meals, entry fees, excursions, study leaders, local guides, pre-trip material, reading lists. National Trust membership: individual $20, family $24.

What it costs:
$2,965 for 6 days, historic Savannah and Charleston
$2,795 for 9 days, village life in Wales
$5,140 for 17 days, Morocco
$7,500 and up for international cruises and private jet tours

"The guest lecturers were excellent and our guide was one in a million." Couple on tour to Egypt.

North Cascades Institute

Contact: Ruthy Porter, Seminar Coordinator
Address: 2105 Highway 20
Sedro Woolley WA 98284
Phone: 206-856-5700 ext.209
Fax: 206-856-1934
Email: nci@ncascades.org
Web: www.ncascades.org

Outdoor seminars that introduce participants to the beautiful scenery of Washington's North Cascades region are the specialty of the Institute which was founded to increase awareness and stewardship of Pacific Northwest environments. Participants hike to Swakane Canyon to observe butterflies, backpack to the Pasayten Wilderness to read poetry and prose amid the mountains, and hike to the Lake Chelan-Sawtooth Wilderness Area to look for wildflowers and other plants.

"We strive for small, informal classes, bringing together interested and eager learners. Our instructors are expert teachers who take delight in sharing their expertise," notes Saul Weisberg, Executive Director. "We seek to increase understanding and appreciation of the natural, historical, and cultural legacy of the North Cascades."

Founded in 1986, the Institute offers dozens of mostly two or three-day courses year-round related to the region on birds, bugs and butterflies, cultural history, sky, land and seas, flowers, trees and flora, literary arts, mammals, and visual and cultural arts. Topics covered include Raven Ecology and Mythology, Hawks in the Highlands, Beaches of Whidbey, Wildflowers of Sagebrush Country, Wild Edibles and Traditional Uses of Native Plants, Naturalist's Creative Journal, Drum-making Workshop, Mountain Landscape Photography, Diving into Watercolor, and Native American Art & Landscape.

More than 35,000 people, including those in schools and youth programs, internship and volunteer training, and workshops for teachers and professional educators, have taken seminars since the Institute began. Elderhostel courses are offered to seniors as part of the Lifelong Learning Adventures program, and week-long canoe camps for young people in July.

What you get: Some accommodations, some meals, campsite, instruction, equipment. Participants are responsible for food and transportation on some programs.

What it costs:
$165 for 2 days, Mountain Landscape Photography
$175 for 2 days, Raven Ecology and Mythology
$395-$525 for 4 days, Spring Naturalist's Retreat, includes lunches.

"The orca whales show up, serene and formidable. The only wakeful one spy-hops, displaying white saddle patches, dazzling as the snow patches on nearby Mount Derby. They submerge, and reappear behind us spitting vapors. Their dorsal fins rise like curved monoliths. Then the pod moves away from us and we, a pod of humans, wistfully nose our kayaks back to Telegraph Cove."

Northern Lights Expeditions

Contact: David Arcese, President
Address: PO Box 4289
Bellingham WA 98227
Phone: 360-734-6334
800-754-7402
Email: info@seakayaking.com
Web: www.seakayaking.com

David Arcese knows that a close encounter with whales is one of the thrills of sea kayak trips along the Inside Passage, the thousand-mile-long sheltered waterway for vessels traveling between the Northwest up the British Columbia coast to Alaska. Since 1983, his company has specialized in taking people with little or no outdoor experience into an area of exceptional wilderness beauty to observe whales and other animals in their natural surroundings.

You don't have to know how to paddle a kayak or swim. The kayaks are extremely easy to maneuver. Groups explore the hundreds of islands and waterways of the Northwest where killer whales come in the summer months as they follow the millions of salmon swimming to the rivers to spawn.

Every trip has three leaders, experienced kayakers who are knowledgeable about the wildlife of the region. You camp at beautiful sites, eat delicious fresh-cooked meals, often featuring fish caught that day, and find berries ripe for eating on bushes.

Non-campers can stay at a lodge or charter the Northern Lights yacht for a live-aboard kayak journey.

What you get: Accommodations, all meals, transportation, guides, instruction, equipment, pre-trip material, reading lists.

What it costs:
$1,295 for 6 days, camp and kayak, Inside Passage
$1,795 for 6 days, lodge and kayak, Farewell Harbour
$1,995 for 7 days, yacht and kayak, Spirit Bear

"I still have wondrous and remarkable memories, especially the amazing sounds of the pod of orcas passing the islands about midnight. Incredible!" A participant from New York.

Up close to an orca whale

Overseas Adventure Travel

Contact: Information Office
Address: One Broadway, Suite 600
               Cambridge MA 02142
Phone: 800-221-0814
               800-955-1925
Fax: 617-876-0455
Web: www.oattravel.com

"We'll immerse you in an authentic cultural experience," notes Mary B. Marks, OAT senior vice president. "We limit every OAT group to never more than 10 to 16 travelers so we have access to local schoolhouses, small villages, and the homes of our overseas friends."

Since 1979, Overseas Adventure Travel has offered adventure travel to Africa, Asia, Europe, South America, and other Pacific Rim countries. Its trip leaders are expert staff members who often live in the regions that are visited and know the local customs and procedures.

In Africa, OAT offers safaris to Botswana and Zimbabwe to see the Okavango Delta and Victoria Falls as well as spot rhinos, hippos, elephants, buffalos, and lions. On the Serengeti tour you see views of Mount Kilimanjaro, baobab trees, incredible bird life in the Great Rift Valley, and the Olduvai Gorge, where Louis and Mary Leakey discovered early hominid fossil fragments of *Homo habilis,* evidence of early humans. OAT is endorsed by the African Wildlife Foundation because of its strong commitment to conservation.

Other trips travel to Morocco's Atlas Mountains and the towns of Fez, Marrakech, and Casablanca, as well as a stay at a tented camp in the Sahara. In Asia you explore Thailand, with a cooking demonstration at a Thai house; in China you sail down the Yangtze River, and in Nepal, you trek ancient trails in the Himalaya, ride elephants, and visit elementary schools. In South America, you visit Macchu Picchu, the Amazon jungle, the Galapagos Islands, and in Central America, explore the natural world of Costa Rica.

Through OAT's non-profit Grand Circle Foundation, funds are given to worldwide community, cultural, and environmental causes. Since 1992 the Foundation has donated $7 million in support of the Himalayan Trust, World Monuments Fund, SOS Children's Village Portugal, Traditional Textiles of Peru, the Black Rhino Breeding Program, and other programs.

What you get: Airfare round-trip from U.S., accommodations, most meals, transportation, guides, excursions, fees, pre-trip material.

What it costs:
$1,590 for 12 days, Real Affordable Costa Rica
$2,890 for 18 days, Nepal: A Cultural Odyssey
$4,790 for 19 days, The Best of Kenya and Tanzania

"The trip definitely exceeded my expectations. In our small group we were able to see the past, present and future of China. The home visits gave great insight into what people really do and how they live." Woman from Florida on China trip.

River Travel Center

Contact: Annie LeRoy
Address: 214 Main Street
         Point Arena CA 95468
Phone: 800-882-7238
Fax: 707-882-2638
Web: www.rivers.com

Helping travelers arrange raft, kayak, sea kayak and adventure trips to "the most beautiful and spectacular places on our planet" is the mission of this company.

River Travel Center is a travel agency that specializes in rafting and kayaking. It provides information on thousands of trips both in the United States and abroad. You can ask about trips to sea kayak in Alaska's Glacier Bay, raft on the Snake River through Hells Canyon in Idaho, paddle through the Grand Canyon under its incredible cliffs, or explore the exciting Futaleufu River in Chile, among dozens of other options.

A telephone call to the Center's 800 number is an excellent way to start planning an adventure vacation and to book your trip. River Travel Center has details on space available, trip difficulty, water level, costs, special interest tours, how to get there, what you need to bring, and more.

What you get: Accommodations on the water, transportation, all meals, excursions, guides, instruction, equipment, entry fees. Special diets available.

What it costs:
$995 for 7 days, sea kayaking, Mexico
$2,463 for 13 days, rafting Grand Canyon, Arizona
$2,500 for 10 days, rafting, Futaleufu River, Chile

"I would like to applaud and commend the wonderful staff of River Travel Center who so patiently helped us plan and coordinate this trip." Participant from Tucson, Arizona.

"Everything went very smoothly and we really do appreciate the hassle-free vacation." Participant from Nashville, Tennessee.

"The only way to travel! Villages skipped, towns and cities jumped, always somebody else's horizon. O bliss!"
Kenneth Graham.

Rocky Mountain River Tours

Contact: Sheila & Dave Mills
Address: PO Box 8596
Boise ID 83707
Phone: 208-345-2400
Summer: 208-756-4808
Fax: 208-345-2688
Email: rockymtn@micron.net
Web: www.rafttrips.com

Rafting Idaho's Middle Fork of the Salmon River with this company is a joyous experience and all you need bring on the trip are a toothbrush and a smile. Everything else is provided. Dave and Sheila welcome calls for information at any time. Says Dave, "Our motto is there are no strangers here, only friends who have never met."

Sheila and Dave Mills established their company in 1978. Dave is a native of Idaho and has been rafting for 32 years. Sheila is from Montana and is the author of three nationally distributed cookbooks.

The Middle Fork of the Salmon, in the heart of Idaho, runs 105 miles within the largest road-free wilderness, Frank Church River of No Return. The crystal clear water has no motor vessels, crowds or mosquitoes but offers hot springs, 80 major rapids, and trout fishing.

The meals are always outstanding and the Dutch oven menus include Maple Glazed Grilled King Salmon with Dijon Mustard Mashed Potatoes, Spicy Pesto Lasagna, and Sinfully Sumptuous Sticky Buns.

What you get: Accommodations, all meals, transportation, guides, equipment, instruction, entry fees, pre-trip material.

What it costs:
$995 for 4 days, river trip, spring
$1,350 for 5 days, river trip, fall
$$1,625 to $1,765 for 6 days, summer season

"We had a blast — the fishing, kayaking, hiking and rafting were terrific, the food and scenery were out of this world. Most importantly, you've given us perspective on the important stuff in life." Couple from New York City.

Idaho Governor Cecil L. Andrus (far right) and river rafters relax by the Middle Fork of the Salmon River, Idaho

Saga Holidays

Contact: Road Scholar Program
Address: 222 Berkeley Street
Boston MA 02116
Phone: 800-621-2151
800-343-0273
Web: www.sagaholidays.com

"Our mission is to provide adults with high-quality, stimulating learning experiences in fascinating cities, towns, and regions around the world," notes a staff member. "A central goal of the program is to make the history and culture of the places you visit come alive. There are no tests or exams, just enriching educational experiences."

In the almost 50 years since it was founded in Great Britain, Saga Holidays has developed hundreds of tours around the world designed exclusively for travelers age 50 and over. Rather than work with travel agents, Saga mails its brochures directly to travelers who book their vacations via telephone. In Britain, the company has twice been awarded the prestigious Queen's Award for Export Achievement.

A recently introduced Road Scholar Program offers travel tours related to the fine arts, history and civilization, and nature and the environment. To enhance the travel experience, each program involves an educational partner who contributes to the content of the tour. The Mediaeval Murder Mystery program is designed in conjunction with members of the Crime Writers Association in Britain, while the Spanish Masters and Modernists tour offers insight from the Catalan Association of Art Critics.

In France, you follow the footsteps of Impressionist painters Monet, Van Gogh, and Cezanne, In Newfoundland, Canada, you visit an ongoing archaeological dig and learn the techniques of excavation, preservation, and the cataloging of findings. In Japan, the program includes insights into the hidden world of the geisha. A week in Iceland explores one of the most geologically diverse countries in the world.

What you get: Airfare (varies with city), accommodations, most meals, transportation, program director, lecturers, activities, guided tours, excursions, fees, insurance, pre-trip information.

What it costs:
$1,599 for 12 nights, Spanish Masters & Modernists, Spain
$1,799 for 10 nights, Great Chateaux and Wines, France
$1,999 for 8 nights, History & Ecology, Iceland

"The best and most striking feature was the enthusiasm of the lecturers and their depth of proficiency in their subject matter." Participant from Washington, D.C.

"High quality over all. A good combination of general interest items and more specialized subjects." Participant from Texas.

Sea Quest Expeditions

Contact: Mark Lewis, Director
Address: PO Box 2424
             Friday Harbor WA 98250
Phone: 360-378-5767
Email: zoetic@ sea-quest-kayak.com
Web: sea-quest-kayak.com/zoetic.htm

"Imagine yourself in a kayak flowing down a broad ribbon of blue water. Suddenly, they appear. A pod of 20 orcas or killer whales, their six-foot dorsal fins cutting straight for your group. Your senses are filled with their awesome presence. A seven-ton bull harmlessly breaches amid a thunderous splash. Glistening black-and-white hulks gently glide through your flotilla without so much as rocking a single kayak. Gradually the family of whales rounds the point and leaves your sight — but the memory stays with you forever."

Mark Lewis leads kayak trips to explore premier whale and wildlife habitat in the world, and believes that the best way to observe whales is in a non-intrusive manner. He leads sea kayak tours to areas where you can observe large whales swim close by, in the waters of the San Juan Islands of Washington, the Gulf of California, the glacial fjords of southeast Alaska, and in British Columbia, Canada. All expeditions include a biologist on staff to enhance the understanding of the marine environment.

"Our paddling routes are carefully planned to traverse the most important whale habitats," notes Lewis. "Our skilled biologist guides have years of experience to help them bring about an encounter."

As well as trips, the company offers a marine sciences program for teens, a sea kayak skills class, and a program on the ecology of marine mammals. Custom trips can also be arranged.

Zoetic Research is the small non-profit arm of the company that operates Sea Quest Expeditions. Its activities include outdoor environmental education, scientific investigation, and financial support for leading conservation groups. Part of the fees from trips is donated to groups dedicated to preserving natural areas and wildlife.

What you get: Accommodations, all meals, transportation, entry fees, guides, equipment, instruction, pre-trip material, reading lists, insurance.

What it costs:
$59 for one day, San Juan Islands, Washington.
$549 for 5 days, San Juan Islands, Washington.
$1,059 for 8 days, Baja California, Mexico.
$1,809 for 9 days, Glaciers & Whales, Southeast Alaska.

"Your incredible expertise and concern for excellence made the trip truly outstanding." Participant from Minnesota.

Sea Turtle Restoration Project

Contact: Randall Aranz
Address: PO Box 400
Forest Knolls CA 94933
Phone: 415-488-0370
800-859-SAVE
Fax: 415-488-0372
Email: rarauz@sol.racsa.co.cr
Web: www.seaturtles.org

Turtle-lovers can vacation for two weeks or a month relaxing on beautiful beaches in Costa Rica between July and December and help preserve the endangered olive ridley turtles who nest there. You may even see an *arribada* or synchronized nesting of thousands and thousands of turtles at the same time, which occurs on only nine beaches worldwide.

"Watching an ancient sea turtle rumble out of the surf and lay her eggs is an experience of a lifetime. It's like peering back into the time of the dinosaurs," says director Todd Steiner.

The Pacific Costa Rica sites are San Miguel in Guanacaste, Punta Banco and Cana Blanca, in the southern region of the country, close to the Panama border. These projects are carried out at Olive Ridley solitary nesting beaches, where 200 to 300 or more turtles nest during this five-month season. Occasional Pacific green turtles, leatherbacks, and hawksbills are also recorded each year.

No expertise or experience is necessary - you are taught all you need to know and are accompanied by a staff member. This is part of a real research project. Be prepared to walk several miles on the beaches at night in hot, humid, and possibly rainy weather. There's also time to hike, visit tidepools, swim, and bird watch during the day.

You can stay at the Tiskita Lodge, a comfortable Costa Rican family-run lodge in the rain forest with rustic cabins and views of the rocky Pacific coast, share an ocean-front community cabin in the middle of the town, or stay in the group's station.

STRP is also working to establish the Kemp's Ridley Marine Reserve off the coast of Texas to prohibit shrimp fishing and protect endangered sea turtles and other marine life. Ridley turtles and other species of turtles are struggling to survive worldwide. The number of nesting leatherback turtles at Playa Grande in Costa Rica, for example, dropped from 1,367 to only 117 in recent years.

What you get: Accommodations, all meals, day trips, guides, instruction, pre-trip material, reading lists.

What it costs:
$650 for 14 nights, Community Cabins, Punta Banco
$850 for 28 days, Community Cabins, Punta Banco
$900 for 14 nights package, Tiskita Lodge, Punta Banco

"Great opportunity for people to travel, learn, and be involved in change for the better." A participant.

Seniors Abroad
International Homestay

Contact: Evelyn Zivetz, Director
Address: 12533 Pacato Circle North
San Diego CA 92128
Phone: 858-485-1696
Fax: 858-487-1492
Email: haev@pacbell.net

Seniors Abroad arranges homestays for people age 50 and over in Japan, New Zealand, Australia, England, Scotland, and Wales.

"Hosts and guests write to each other before they meet, and the guests are welcomed as members of the host family," notes Zivetz, who started the company to encourage people to learn alternative ways to stay active in their later years. Hospitality is volunteered on the part of the host and without cost to the guest. All programs can be extended for independent travel.

Founded in 1984, several programs are offered. A month's trip to New Zealand and Australia includes five different homestays and a four-night hotel stay for orientation. On a tour of England, Scotland, and Wales for three weeks, there are three homestays and two nights in a hotel. On a three-week tour of Japan there are three homestays and three nights in a hotel.

Americans who don't want to travel can volunteer to host a couple or a single person from abroad for six days.

What you get: Airfare, accommodations, transportation, most meals, hospitality with families.

What it costs:
$2,400 for 21 days, England, Scotland, Wales
$2,600 for 28 days, Japan
$3,500 for 28 days, New Zealand & Australia

"Over the years, when our children were home, we hosted younger people from abroad. Now Seniors Abroad gives us the opportunity to host persons of our own age." Couple from Australia.

"You see more by staying with senior citizens because they give you the insight. You learn to know their country, their customs, and they take you everywhere." Participant from Florida.

"It is not money which travel demands so much as leisure, and anyone with a small, fixed income can travel all the time." Frank Tatchell

Smithsonian Study Tours

Contact: Prudence Clendenning/Amy Kotkin
Address: 1100 Jefferson Drive SW, Suite 3077
Washington DC 20560-0702
Phone: 202-357-4700
Tollfree 877-338-8687
Fax: 202-786-2536
Email: tours@tsa.si.edu
Web: www.SmithsonianStudyTours.org

Throughout the year Smithsonian offers more than 350 expert-led tours and seminars around the globe. As the largest, most diverse museum-sponsored educational travel program in the world, Smithsonian Study Tours draws on its unequaled resources and contacts to provide special access to the people and places that make their trips unforgettable. Smithsonian participants explore unique and exciting regions from Alaska to Australia, the Mississippi River to the Mediterranean Sea, and from Japanese teahouses to African galleries. Study topics range from the California Gold Rush to the design of English gardens, preserving wildlife to creating sculpture, and performing arts in Russia to the birds of Chesapeake Bay.

Jennifer Beltz

On a Grand Canyon Family Adventure trip, travelers look out over the rim of the canyon in Arizona

Smithsonian Study Tours are carefully designed to provide participants with the most rewarding travel adventure for every taste, interest, and budget. Smithsonian travelers may choose from any of the following types of offerings:

US and Canada Study Tours offer both outdoor adventures and cultural journeys where travelers can choose from a variety of activities including exploring the majestic Yellowstone wildlife in winter, or studying the Native cultures of the Southwest. Others may choose to hike on Hawaii's cliff trails and sandy beaches, follow in the footsteps of Lewis and Clark, or visit the picturesque landscapes of the Hudson River Valley.

Seminars present unique single-focus programs ranging from the Civil War, to astronomy in Arizona, and art and performing arts programs, including theater and music at the Spoleto Festival USA. Other seminars highlight regional cuisines. Opera lovers can enjoy behind the scenes visits and operas at the Metropolitan Opera, Santa Fe Opera and in Italy and France. Others can become a student during our Annual Oxford Seminar, and some can experience the conflict of WWI during a new program in France.

Odyssey Tours are designed for travelers looking to maximize enjoyment and minimize costs. Visit popular destinations and choose from a selection of departure dates. Whether you tour the cultural treasures of Spain or discover the natural wonders of Borneo, Smithsonian Odyssey Tours offers unprecedented value air and land packages.

International Study Tours include a wide array of land-based tours, voyages on the world's great rivers, and ocean passages. Smithsonian voyages employ a variety of small ships from an icebreaker voyage to the North Pole, a cruise to Antarctica; voyages on all the major European rivers as well as China's Yangtze. Land programs range from shorter **Essence and Countryside** tours that take place in one special region, to journeys across China and Central Asia to Istanbul. All feature expert leadership including one or more study leader, tour manager and the best local guides.

What you get: Accommodations, transportation, most meals, excursions, gratuities, comprehensive lecture program by Smithsonian study leader, pre-trip material, reading list.

What it costs:
$1,899 for 10 days, Western Canada & National Parks (with Saga)
$2,450 for 8 days, Hiking in Yellowstone & Beartooth Mountains, Montana
$3,935 for 8 days in England, Christmas in Bath
$6,195 for 10 days in Paris, Opera Lover's France

"We get to travel with like-minded people who are intelligent and have a curiosity about the world. Over the years we've developed a network of friends who take these trips." Participant from Oklahoma.

"My soul grows a little bit each time I take a Smithsonian tour. They are not vacations; they are personal journeys of exploration and adventure." Participant on Utah Red Rocks tour.

Spirit of India

Contact: · Barbara Sansone
Address: PO Box 446
Mill Valley CA 94942
Phone: 415-381-5861
888-367-6147
Email: inquire@spirit-of-india.com
Web: www.spirit-of-india.com

"India is like no place you have ever been," explains director Barbara Sansone. "It is bursting with sights, sounds, smells and pulsating energy. The land is exotic, the people colorful, warm and friendly, the organizational system — complete chaos!"

Exploring educational, cultural, and spiritual India with carefully selected guides who are scholars and professional experts is the company's speciality. Sansone, a former educator and editorial photographer creates trips that enable you to travel comfortably and avoid the hassles which solo travelers often encounter.

You can explore north India's diverse range of arts and architecture with guide Dr. Donald Stadtner, Ph. D. in Indian Art History, University of California-Berkeley, where you stay in palaces, luxury hotels and heritage properties to

A sunset camel ride in the desert of Jodhpur in Rajastan, India, during the annual Pushkar Camel Faire

Barbara Sansone

visit ancient mosques, rare Dilwara Jain temples, the Taj Mahal, the Crafts Museum of Delhi, and the Elephanta, Ajanta and Ellora caves. You also see the exquisite miniature painting in Udaipur, silk and cotton handwoven textiles, and bronze and marble sculptures.

A textile and fashion tour, escorted by British fashion consultant Laura Avery, showcases the rich history and diverse traditional techniques of India's textiles including handwoven silks, block print cottons, tie dye fabrices, embroidery, and beadwork, as well as gold, silver, glass and ceramic jewelry. In the north, south and part of east India, you will visit fashion centers such as Delhi, Jaipur, and Bombay as well as remote villages where the crafts originated. You will meet with the local artisans and have an opportunity to practice some of the artistic techniques.

Spiritual India: A Yoga Journey is led by Mr. Arun Archaya, Sanskrit scholar and yoga master. The Pushkar Camel Faire in Rajasthan is the highlight of another tour that includes four days in a deluxe royal camp near the fair and takes you to explore exotic tribal villages of Rajasthan. There is a camel ride in the desert at sunset.

In the summer, a small group of no more than 12 travelers explores the ancient cultures of Kinnaur and Spiti Valley, remote districts in the Indian Himalya, bordering Tibet. This area has been closed to foreign travelers until recently. You travel by jeep and sleep in deluxe tents, visiting villages and ancient monasteries at the top of the world. You will be invited to tea by the head lama of one monastery, participate in morning chanting with the monks, and admire the pristine beauty of the scenery.

What you get: Airfare from US on most tours, accommodations, transportation, entry fees, specialized guides, guest presenters, pre-trip material, reading lists, most meals. Vegetarian diets available.

What it costs:
$4,785 for 19 days, Pushkar Camel Faire, India.
$4,885 for 20 days, Art & Architecture, North India.
$4,975 for 23 days, Spiritual India: A Yoga Journey

"Sensational! It was so well organized, great service, we met such interesting people and the places we stayed at were first-class. A wonderful trip." Couple from Boston on Art & Architecture in North India tour.

"It was the most wonderful trip. We spent a week in a monastery in the north, and were part of a special millennium ceremony with more than 10,000 people from all over the world where the Dalai Lama spoke. It was an amazing experience." TV network operations manager from Brooklyn, NY on Spiritual India tour.

The World Outdoors

Contact: Brian T. Mullis, Director
Address: 2840 Wilderness Place, Suite F
Boulder CO 80301
Phone: 303-413-0938
800-488-8483
Fax: 303-413-0926
Email: Fun@theworldoutdoors.com
Web: www.theworldoutdoors.com

Adventure trips year-round to discover the wonders of nature on little known trails and waterways are offered by this company, formerly called Roads Less Traveled, with groups of no more than 13 and a guide-to-guest ratio of one to seven.

Among the beautiful places you can explore is the Grand Canyon with a hiking trip into the canyon to visit Havasu. You can also see the Grand Canyon on a multi-sport hiking and biking trip that also visits Bryce, and Zion on a week-long camping trip.

There's a hiking, biking, rafting and horseback riding multi-sport tour of the Grand Tetons and Yellowstone National Park in Wyoming where you stay at inns or camp. You can try sea kayaking and snorkeling as well as hike and bike in the Yucatan on the Caribbean, or take a hiking trip through the Canadian Rockies with views of beautiful mountains and lakes. Other trips explore Alaska, Yosemite, Rocky Mountain National Park, New Mexico, Hawaii, Belize, Guatemala, Cuba, Dominican Republic, Baja, Peru, Costa Rica, Australia, and New Zealand, and there are special camping trips available for families.

"Active travel — traveling under your own power and at your own pace — is the best way to return home refreshed, renewed and revitalized," notes a staff person. "Whatever your level of fitness, we have a trip that fits your needs."

What you get: Accommodations, transportation, entry fees, excursions, guides, some equipment, instruction, pre-trip material, reading lists, all meals. Special diets available.

What it costs:
$995-$1,595 for 6 days, Colorado Multi-Sport.
$1,595 for 6 days, Grand Canyon Hiker, singles.
$1,795 for 7 days, Yucatan-Caribbean Multi-Sport.

"The experience allowed me to break away from the real world and explore the beauty of Colorado. It exceeded all my expectations." Participant from New York, Colorado Multi-Sport

"I really appreciated the support and encouragement offered by the guides. Their patience and assistance helped stretch the limits of what I thought I was capable of." Participant from California, Teton-Yellowstone Multi-Sport

TraveLearn

Contact: Keith M. Williams
Address: PO Box 315
Lakeville PA 18438
Phone: 800-235-9114
Fax: 570-226-6912
Email: keith@travelearn.com
Web: www.travelearn.com

Company director and founder, Professor Edwin Williams, is a former director of international studies at Kean College of New Jersey and began leading trips to Kenya in the 1970s. He has personally escorted travel study programs in Kenya, China, Egypt, Morocco, and the Galapagos Islands and Ecuador. Groups average 14 participants.

"The hallmarks of TraveLearn's programs are the on-site lectures, seminars, and field experiences conducted by local resource specialists in co-operation with an accompanying faculty escort," he notes. "Adult learners have contact with local people, and have the opportunity to visit sites and facilities often not available to the average tourist on conventional tours."

His trips offer learning vacations for educated travelers and adult learners to 18 worldwide destinations. Every trip is supervised by college faculty specialists, and travel programs are marketed by continuing education services at more than 300 universities in 45 states and 4 countries.

Trips to the Galapagos Islands, Ecuador, and to Costa Rica include a meal with a local family, for a firsthand discussion on environmental and other issues. The China Odyssey program includes tours of Beijing and visits to factories, farms, and schools in five cities. The program in Egypt includes a slide seminar by the Director of Antiquities at Giza, a lecture on the changing role of women in Egyptian society, and a cruise along the Nile.

What you get: Airfare from U.S., transportation, accommodations, most meals, entry fees, excursions, guides, instruction, pre-trip materials, reading lists.

What it costs:
$2,295 for 14 days, Inside Passage Cruise, Alaska
$2,995 for 17 days, Peoples Republic of China
$4,095 for 14 days, Galapagos Islands and Ecuador

"I appreciated the professionalism of TraveLearn in coordinating the program, and our guide, whose knowledge of ancient Egypt and insight into present day Egypt was an intense credit course at a university." Participant from Arizona.

"I enjoyed the wide variety of experience we were offered in China, from huge city sight-seeing to the small village street dancing. A great trip!" Participant from New York.

Tuscan Way

Contact: Isabel Innocenti, Director
Address: 2829 Bird Avenue, #242
Coconut Grove FL 33133
Phone: 305-446-0127
800-766-2390
Fax: 305-448-2086
Email: Tuscanway@aol.com
Web: www.tuscanway.com

Visit Italy's beautiful southern Tuscany, far from the tourist route, and enjoy a vacation with vineyards and cypress trees, charming villages, and superb food and wine while you stay in a wonderful old villa as guests of the family.

Tuscan Way offers seven-day and four-day cooking courses as well as spa vacations, wine tours, and cycling and hiking trips based in Tuscany. You stay in Casa Innocenti, the picturesque medieval home of the chef and host, Carlo Innocenti, in the village of Arcidosso. The house dates back to A.D. 1100 and its five stories give you views of the piazza, the castle and Monte Amiata, the highest mountain of the region.

Carlo teaches *la cucina povera*, or peasant cuisine, a relaxed, informal style of cooking with a glass of local wine always within arm's reach. No more than eight guests attend and you learn to prepare an array of seasonal dishes including soups, traditional holiday cakes, vegetables, seafood, sauces with mushrooms and truffles, and chestnuts and game meats in the fall.

You visit local markets, restaurants, and vineyards, and learn which wines to serve. Other excursions take you to Montalcino and its vineyards, to Sovana and Pitigliano to see ancient ghettos and Etruscan tombs, and to the seaside village of Castiglione della Pescaia.

What you get: Accommodations, all meals, wine, transportation, airport transfers, excursions, guides, equipment, instruction, tips. Special diets available.

What it costs:
$1,240 for 4 days, per person double, Cooking Course.
$1,400 for 7 days, per person double, Spa Vacation Saturnia.
$2,290 for 7 days, per person double, Wine Tour.

"I left my heart on a hill in Tuscany. Believe me when I tell you on behalf of all of us, that we never had a more wonderful trip in our lives." Woman from Atlanta, GA.

"Venice is like eating an entire box of chocolate liqueurs at one go."   Truman Capote

UC Research Expeditions Program

Contact: Director UREP
Address: University of California-Davis
One Shields Avenue, Davis CA 95616
Phone: 530-752-0692
Fax: 530-752-0681
Email: urep@ucdavis.edu
Web: http://urep.ucdavis.edu

If you'd like to work alongside University of California scientists as they study specific projects related to the environment, you can vacation in exotic locations such as Venezuela, Argentina, Kenya, Nepal, Belize, Chile, Israel, Indonesia and South Africa.

The mission of UREP, established in 1976, is to improve our understanding of life on earth through partnerships between University of California researchers and members of the general public.

You apply to UREP for the project that interests you from the catalog, and if selected, you become an active member of the research team and contribute an equal share to cover the project's cost. No special academic or field experience is necessary to participate. Curiosity, adaptability, and willingness to share the costs and lend a helping hand are the most important qualifications.

In Belize, you help study the least-known and most endangered groups of mammals, medium sized carnivores including jaguarundi and ocelot, and assist by capturing and tagging prey species. In Hungary, you will be part of an international effort to unearth Bronze Age artifacts hidden beneath large earth mounds along the Danube River. In Venezuela's central wetlands, you study Orinoco geese by locating and monitoring nests in natural tree cavities, and help with capturing and banding the birds.

In the United States, you assist research into the delicate ecology of the Arizona desert as the climate changes and as exotic species displace native desert flora. In Jackson Hole, Wyoming, you study the gradual shifting of the Teton Range to see if it is gradually rising by recording changes in the height of mountains.

What you get: Accommodations, all meals, transportation, camping and field gear, research equipment and supplies, reading lists, instruction. Participants make a tax-deductible donation to cover costs.

What it costs:
$895 for 10 days, Chihuahuan Desert, Arizona
$1,395 for 2 weeks, Saving Orinoco Geese, Venezuela
$1,535 for 2 weeks, Slave Traders of Lake Nyasa, Malawi

"It was a wonderful introduction to archaeological field work. I'm hooked for life." Business woman participant.

"One of the most educational and fun experiences of my life." Retired woman participant.

University of California — Berkeley

Contact: Lynne Kaufman & Tanya Nygaard
Address: Travel With Scholars
55 Laguna Street
Berkeley CA 94102
Phone: 415-252-5229
888-209-7344
Fax: 415-252-5285
Email: tln@unx.berkeley.edu
Web: www.unex.berkeley.edu/travel

Students, professionals, and retirees join Berkeley's Travel With Scholars study programs to England, China, France, and Italy among others with the focus on arts, culture, and history led by outstanding experts in the field.

One of the most popular is the joint summer program with Oxford University, England. Two three-week sessions offer a variety of courses including Shakespeare; The Tragedies, English Gardens in History, English Detective Story, Roman Britain, Writers and their Craft, and Castles and Country Houses among others. Students have access to the university libraries, museums, and gardens of the college.

Since the program began in 1979, more than 5,000 people have taken part.

Other programs take travelers to Paris for courses on Photographing Paris and Decorative Arts, to Southwestern France to study caves and castles, to Florence and Tuscany to explore art and architecture, to China to travel on the Yangtze River, to Ireland to study Mythic Patterns in Literature and Culture, and to London for a Theater Scene program with attendance at 12 performances.

What you get: Accommodations, transportation, some airfares, entry fees, excursions, guides, instructions, tips, reading lists, most meals. Special diets available.

What it costs:
$3,500 for 3 weeks, Paris, France
$3,750 for 3 weeks, Oxford University, England
$5,450 for 18 days, China and the Yangtze

"Wonderful, stimulating experience in a beautiful and historic setting with interesting people." Participant from California at Oxford University.

University of New Orleans

Contact: Irene B. Ziegler, Program Specialist
Address: Division of International Education
Metropolitan College UNO
New Orleans LA 70148-2560
Phone: 504-286-7116/7318
Fax: 504-280-7317
Email: iziegler@uno.edu
Web: www.uno.edu/~inst/tmc

The cornerstone of UNO's international study program is its successful relationship with the University of Innsbruck in Austria. The university, located amid the spectacular mountains of the Tyrolean Alps and on the banks of the Inn River, has signed a Friendship Treaty with UNO and two other universities so that UNO students are accepted at Innsbruck. The Innsbruck University buildings are a few minutes walk from the Old City, which dates back to Roman times. The town is within easy reach of Munich, Venice, Florence, and Rome.

In the summer, adult students can take courses for three weeks in July. These include Fiction, Music and Movies: Modern European Intersections, Austria in the Heart of Europe, and a program on language and culture with German conversation classes and excursions. The area has outstanding hiking, and tennis and golf facilities for leisure time.

Another summer program for college-age students and adults is focused on music. The Three Musical Cities: Vienna, Salzburg, and Prague takes students to all three cities to learn their history, explore, and listen to music. Morning classes are followed by afternoon excursions with guides, as well as free days for sight-seeing. Performances include Mozart's *Don Giovanni* at the Vienna State Opera and Bizet's *Carmen* in the National Theater of Prague.

What you get: Accommodations, most meals, transportation passes, tuition, facilities, activities, tickets to performances, entrance fees, excursions, tips, guides, insurance.

What it costs:
$2,695 for 20 days, Three Musical Cities
$3,295 for 21 days, European Centre, Innsbruck, Austria

"The whole program is extremely organized. We were well briefed before leaving on our trips, and there is no earthly way I could have done so much and seen so much on my own. The European Center rates a 9.9!" Participant from Louisiana at European Centre.

University of Pennsylvania

Contact: Elizabeth Sachs, Penn Summer Abroad
Address: 3440 Market Street, Suite 100
Philadelphia PA 19104-3335
Phone: 215-898-5738
Fax: 215-573-2053

Social sciences, culture and language programs are offered by the University of Pennsylvania's Penn Summer Abroad seminars in Argentina, Czech Republic, England, France, Germany, India, Italy, Korea, Poland, Russia, Spain, and Tanzania.

In Poland, students study at the Warsaw School of Economics, with the aim of understanding the social, economic, and political problems of a society in transition to democracy. The course includes classes and short-term internships. In Prague, the program includes the Czech language, Central European civilization, and a special course on Jewish studies in collaboration with the Jewish Museum of Prague.

In France, one of the programs takes place at the University of Bordeaux, near the famous fossil and pre-history sites of Lascaux and Cro-Magnon. Field trips there and to other sites are an important part of the course, which examines the beginnings of modern humankind.

In India, students attend classes at the University of Pune campus, and study Indian religions and philosophies, performing arts, business world and investments, and traditional medicine. In addition, students are required to take part in a community project and to seek internships with affiliated local museums, industries, or hospitals.

Spanish language, literature, and culture courses are offered in Alicante, Spain, near the famous Playa de San Juan beach. You spend the first week visiting Madrid, Segovia, Toledo, and Granada and take classes four days a week in Alicante while staying with local families. Courses include beginner and intermediate Spanish, advanced composition, Spanish culture and civilization, and contemporary Spanish literature.

What you get: Accommodations, some meals, excursions, tuition, reading lists.

What it costs:
$2,150 for 3 weeks, Bordeaux, France.
$4,850 for 5 weeks, Alicante, Spain.
$5,170 for 6 weeks, Pune, India. (incl. airfare from New York).

"The trip really opened my eyes to the beauty of Indian culture: the families, the classes, the art, the dance, the poetry, the religion, the cuisine, the shopping district, all played a crucial role in unfolding the diversity that is India." Participant on Penn-in-India program.

University of Rhode Island

Contact: Professor Mario F. Trubiano
Address: Summer Program in Spain
Dept. of Languages URI
Kingston RI 02881
Phone: 401-792-4717
Fax: 401-874-4694
Web: www.uri.edu/artici/ml/Salamanca.html

Intensive language and cultural programs, as well as a graduate program leading to a master's degree in Hispanic Studies, are offered by the University of Rhode Island in collaboration with the Colegio Hispano Continental in Salamanca, Spain.

The four-week summer courses offer 25 hours a week of classroom instruction, four hours a week of language practice, and 30 hours of excursions and cultural activities. There are two critics-in-residence on hand to answer questions about Spanish literature, society, and culture. Students live with families or in dormitories on campus.

Students join excursions to Segovia, Madrid, Toledo, Leon, Zamora, Avila, Alba de Tormes, and the Andalucian region of Seville, Cordoba, and Granada, and also visit Galicia and

Santiago. They attend a literary colloquium with novelist Ana Maria Matute.

What you get: Accommodations, all meals, transportation, tuition, cultural activities, three excursions with guide, language practicum, parties.

What it costs:
$1,700 for 28 days, Intensive Language Instruction, Spain
$1,750 for 28 days, Graduate & Advanced Courses, Spain

University of Wisconsin — Madison Extension

Contact: Kim Seymour
Address: Performing Arts/Educational Study Tours
              724 Lowell Center, 610 Langdon Street
              Madison WI 53703-1195
Phone: 608-262-3731
Fax: 608-262-1694
Email: kseymour@dcs.wisc.edu
Web: www.dcs.wisc.edu/lsa/travel

A wide array of performing arts/educational study tours is offered by the University of Wisconsin-Madison/Extension. These adult education tour packages vary from a few days to a few weeks and are accompanied by professional and experienced tour directors. Participants do not need to be affiliated with the University of Wisconsin nor be a Wisconsin resident.

Performing Arts Study Tours visit New York, Washington, D.C., San Francisco, Toronto, Montreal, and other major cities to attend opera, dance, music, and theater performances. There are also tours to festivals, including the Shakespeare Festival in Stratford, the Shaw Festival in

Ontario, Canada, and the Spoleto Music Festival in Charleston, South Carolina.

Arts Seminars Abroad Tours enjoy opera, dance, music and theater experiences and include New Year's in London, Spring Week in London, and Fall Week in Dublin. A seminar to the Edinburgh Festival in Scotland is a traditional event.

The Arts Seminars Abroad for Teachers program offers participants the opportunity to earn university credit. Tour destinations have included Rome, Paris, Barcelona, and Brittany. Tours are arranged and accompanied by an expert director/educator and participants are allowed to explore their personal and professional interests.

The Medieval Study Tour program offers educational study tours to several medieval historic sites and locations including France, Ireland, Wales, and England. These tours are led by a medieval historian and aim to provide a complete educational experience at each site.

What you get: Accommodations, some meals, transportation, reserved performances, entry fees, excursions, educational seminars, study materials, readings lists, pre-trip materials, professional on-site tour leadership. Special diets available.

What it costs:
$850 for 4 days in New York City (no meals)
$1,650 for 8 days in London
$1,700 for 8 days, Edinburgh Festival, Scotland

Wilderness Travel

Contact: Barbara Banks
Address: 1102 Ninth Street
Berkeley CA 94710
Phone: 510-558-2488
800-368-2794
Fax: 510-558-2489
Email: info@wildernesstravel.com
Web: www.wildernesstravel.com

You float silently down a remote jungle river in the Amazon Basin accompanied by Indian guides. You watch thousands of flamingoes feeding in a shallow lake as dawn spreads across the African sky. You sail from island to island in the Galapagos as dolphins dart alongside the yacht. You hike past remote Buddhist monasteries in the shadow of Mount Everest. You stroll from village to village and enjoy the delicious food and drink of Tuscany on an Italian walk.

These are the images of trips with Wilderness Travel. Established in 1978, the company specializes in mountain treks, adventure sailing, inn-to-inn hiking tours, overland trips, and hotel and camping safaris. Its catalog provides a colorful introduction to more than 90 trips to Africa, the Middle East, Europe, Asia, the Pacific, the Galapagos Islands,

Latin America, and Antarctica. Tour leaders are natural history experts, backcountry guides, scholars, and authors who know the region, speak the local language, and are a critical link with local people who trust them.

They also offer specialized trips such as a look at High Altitude and Tropical Medicine in Nepal for medical professionals, and a trip to Iran to trek in the Elborz Mountains.

There are demanding trips. You can join a strenuous 17-day hike in the high Andes of the Cordillera Blanca in Peru where you see mountain peaks, glaciers, and fascinating villages, or an Everest adventure where you hike trails with spectacular views of the magnificent mountain as you travel a circuit through classic Sherpa villages.

More leisurely tours include a ramble though the sunny Basque country between Spain and France, visiting vineyards, traditional farms, and ancient stone burial monuments, and a trip through the national parks of South Africa to see Bushmen rock art, Zulu battlefields, and white rhinos.

What you get: Accommodations, airfare in country, transportation, entry fees, excursions, guides, equipment, instruction, tips, pre-trip materials, reading lists, most meals. Special diets available.

What it costs:
$2,795 for 13 days, Tour du Mont Blanc, Switzerland
$2,995 for 16 days, Turquoise Coast, Turkey
$4,695 for 15 days, Serengeti Wildlife Safari, Africa

"The ruins and scenery were spectacular, the other travelers interesting, and the yacht and crew were superb." Participant on Turquoise Coast in Turkey sailing.

"What wonderful memories and photos — I'm already trying to figure out when I can return!" Participant on East Africa Wildlife Safari.

Wildland Adventures

Contact: Kurt Kutay
Address: 3516 NE 155th Street
Seattle WA 98155
Phone: 206-365-0686
800-345-4453
Fax: 206-663-6615
Email: info@wildland.com
Web: www.wildland.com

Since 1986, the company has taken small groups, families and individuals on cultural and natural history journeys of personal discovery to enrich their lives and the lives of the people they encounter on their travels. The company's Travelers Conservation Trust, a non-profit organization, supports conservation and community development in host countries.

Comprehensive Travel Planners are provided for all destinations and include itineraries, maps, photographs, departure dates, and suggestions on how to plan the trip that best meets your personal interest and style of travel.

You can visit Alaska, Central America, South America, Africa, Turkey and the Middle East. On a trip to Jordan, you spend time in Amman, the modern and ancient capital, visit a newly developed reserve which protects endangered species, and see the Red-Rose City of Petra. A variety of trips to Costa Rica's parks and reserves take you through the tropical rainforest, to see volcanoes and jungle lodges, and to hike along Caribbean beaches. In Panama, you can visit the Canal, a Tropical Research Marine Center, and a cloud forest reserve to see the Quetzal and other exotic birds. Alaska offers a wildlife odyssey with cruising and sea kayaking, together with hikes to explore the wilderness of Denali NationalPark looking for bald eagles, moose, bear and wolf. In Peru, you hike up the Inca trail to Machu Picchu and its spectacular ruins.

The company has also created a Trees for Travel program where trees are planted around the world to absorb the carbon dioxide created by airplanes.

What you get: Accommodations, airfare in country, transportation, excursions, entry fees, guides, reading lists, pre-trip material, most meals. Special diets available.

What it costs:
$1,895 for 8 days, Tropical Trails Odyssey, Costa Rica.
$2,120 for 10 days, Panama Explorer.
$4,195 for 12 days, Alaska Adventure

"Everything was so far beyond our expectations and imaginings that the whole trip was beyond belief. Thank you so much for such a memorable holiday." Participant on Serengeti Camping Safari, Kilimanjaro Machame Climb.

"Just wanted to inform you that our trip was absolutely brilliant! The Peru part was completely flawless — Machu Picchu is the most beautiful place I've ever seen." Participant on the Andes and Amazon Odyssey, Peru.

World Learning

Contact: Director/Summer Abroad
Address: PO Box 676
Brattleboro VT 05302-0676
Phone: 802-257-7751
800-345-2929
Fax: 802-258-3248
Email: eil@worldlearning.org
Web: www.usexperiment.org

Founded in 1932 as The Experiment in International Living, World Learning offers a variety of ways in which high school students can live abroad and learn about different cultures firsthand.

Thousands of young people have taken part in these exchanges, and students can choose the style of learning they prefer. Homestay and Travel programs in Europe, Africa, Asia, and Latin America, and other countries allow them to live with families abroad and experience total immersion in the language and culture of a single place and people. Community Service programs in Belize, Israel, Kenya, and Thailand involve students who want to make personal contributions in service to communities. Ecological Adventures in

Australia and Ecuador among others tackle international environmental problems.

Homestay: Students live with a family in one of 25 countries including Australia, Belize, Brazil, Ecuador, France, Germany, Great Britain, Japan, Kenya, and Thailand.

Ecological Adventure: By examining a global ecological problem firsthand, students learn how the actions of one country affect the ecology of another.

Community Service: Students can make a personal contribution of service by working on specific projects.

Language Study: Focusing on verbal communications skills, students benefit from experienced teachers in an interactive learning atmosphere in the community.

Extended Travel: In some countries, students can travel for a week following the homestay.

What you get: Airfare, accommodations, all meals, orientation, language training, transportation, excursions, events, admission fees, insurance.

What it costs:
$3,950 for 29 days, Language Study, Costa Rica
$4,700 for 35 days, Ecological Adventure, Australia
$4,900 for 31 days, Homestay and Travel, China
$4,975 for 39 days, Community Service, Kenya

"A man travels the world in search of what he needs and returns home to find it."   George Moore

Yellowstone Association Institute

Contact: Diane Kline, Registrar
Address: PO Box 117
            Yellowstone National Park, WY 82190
Phone: 307-344-2294
Fax: 307-344-2485
Email: dkline@YellowstoneAssociation.org
Web: www.YellowstoneAssociation.org

The Yellowstone Association was founded in 1933 by a group of private citizens who wanted to provide a research library for Yellowstone, which became one of the finest in the National Park system. Since then, the YA has grown to become a major supporter of educational and scientific programs in the park, and also supplements the educational programs offered by the National Park Service through the Yellowstone Association Institute.

The Institute offers more than 120 in-depth educational programs in the Park that last from one to six days and are led by experts in the field. More than 1,800 people take courses every year. You can join a wildlife watch to observe wolves, elk, grizzly bears, and more in the early morning and evening, backpack in the Old Faithful region to see waterfalls and plants unique to the area, learn how to recognize bird songs, join a writing workshop to understand how to capture the magnificent landscape in words, and hike trails to admire spectacular lakes, vistas, and wildflowers. You can learn about drawing birds, bees, butterflies, and botany, go kayaking on Shoshone Lake, study thermal springs for microbial life and how these organisms thrive, look at the fossils of Yellowstone, learn how to be a backyard astronomer, and find out about nature photography amid sweeping landscapes. In winter, there are programs on wilderness first aid, outings to ski and snowshoe in the park, and a program to study the ecology of reading tracks in the snow.

On some programs, rooms and meals are available at hotels in the park. You can also stay at the Lamar Buffalo Ranch Field Campus for $20 a night, which has log guest cabins and a common building, kitchen, and showers, where you bring your own food and sleeping bag. The bunkhouse is a short walk from the sleeping cabins and is the center of activity for the field campus with a a back porch and outside picnic tables for relaxation. You can also stay in park campgrounds or lodgings outside the park.

What you get: Accommodations sometimes, meals sometimes, transportation, equipment, instruction, guides, tours.

What it costs:
$130 for 2 days, Wildflowers and Wildfire, Lamar Buffalo Ranch
$230 for 4 days, Artistic Field Journals, Old Faithful Hotel
$1,495 for 6 days, Horsepack in the Lamar Valley

Evelyn Kaye

Gentoo penguins in Antarctica

"For my part, I travel not to go anywhere but to go. I travel for travel's sake. The great affair is to move."

Robert Louis Stevenson

SECTION 3: RESOURCES

WEB RESOURCES

Travel information on the Internet is overwhelming in its quantity and quality. Here are some sites worth visiting with good information about learning vacations.

www.shawguides.com

Extensive, detailed and up-to-date information about learning vacations around the world.

www. Expedia.com

A useful site for general travel information, airfares, and travel news.

www.frommers.com

Travel guru Arthur Frommer has a magazine, *Budget Travel*, an on-line newsletter, and a website.

www.GORP.com

The acronym stands for Great Outdoor Recreation Pages. Good information about active vacations where you can learn anything from bicycling and trekking to kayaking and skiing.

www.TransitionsAbroad.com

A long established source for information about how to study, work, or teach abroad. They also publish a magazine.

http://travel.state.gov

The State Department site provides information about places to visit and avoid around the world plus consular information, health conditions, and entry regulations.

www.whytravelalone.com

Director Jens Jurgen brings together people who need travel companions through his company, Travel Companions Exchange and also publishes a newsletter.

RECOMMENDED BOOKS

Fodor's Great American Learning Vacations. 2nd edition. Caroline Haberfeld, editor. (Fodors Travel Publications, 1997)

Free Vacations & Bargain Adventures in the USA. 2nd edition. Evelyn Kaye (Blue Panda Publications, 1998)

Peterson's Learning Adventures Around the World. Peter S. Greenberg. (Petersons, 1997)

Smart Vacations: The Travelers Guide to Learning Adventures Abroad. Priscilla Tovey. (St. Martins Press, 1993)

Studying Abroad/Learning Abroad. J. Daniel Hess. (Intercultural Press, 1997)

Vacations That Can Change Your Life. Ellen Lederman. (Sourcebooks, 1998)

U.S. TOURIST BUREAUS

Alabama
800-ALABAMA
334-242-4169
www.touralabama.orgs

Alaska
907-465-2010
www.travelalaska.com

Arizona
800-842-8257
www.arizonaguide.com

Arkansas
800-NATURAL
www.arizonaguide.com

California
800-TOCALIF
916-322-2881
www.gocalif.ca.gov

Colorado
800-COLORADO
www.colorado.com

Connecticut
800-CT-BOUND
www.ctbound.org

Delaware
800-441-8846
www.state.de.us/tourism

Florida
888-7FLA-USA
904-487-1462
www.flausa.com

Georgia
800-VISIT-GA
404-656-3590
www.georgia.com

Hawaii
800-GO-HAWAII
808-923-1811
www.gohawaii.com

Idaho
800-635-7820
208-334-2470
www.visitid.org

Illinois
800-2-CONNECT
www.enjoyillinois.com

Indiana
800-ENJOY-IN
317-232-8860
www.enjoyindiana.com

Iowa
888-472-6035
www.traveliowa.com

Kansas
800-2-KANSAS
www.kansascommerce.com/
0400travel.html

Kentucky
800-225-TRIP
www.tourky.com

Louisiana
800-677-4082
504-342-8119
www.louisianatravel.com

Maine
888-MAINE-45
307-623-0363
www.visitmaine.com

Maryland
800-MDISFUN
www.mdisfun.org

Massachusetts
800-227-MASS
www.massvacation.com

Michigan
888-78-GREAT
517-373-0670
www.michigan.org

Minnesota
800-657-3700
612-296-5029
www.exploreminnesota.com

Mississippi
800-WARMEST
601-359-3297
www.visitmississippi.org

Missouri
800-877-1234
573-751-4133
www.missouritourism.org

Montana
800-VISIT-MT
406-444-2654
www.visitmt.com

Nebraska
800-228-4307
402-471-3796
www.visitnebraska.org

Nevada
800-NEVADA8
www.travelnevada.com

New Hampshire
800-FUN-IN-NH
603-271-2343
www.visitnh.com

New Jersey
800-VISIT-NJ
609-292-2470
www.state.nj.us/travel

New Mexico
800-SEE-NEWMEX
www.newmexico.org

New York
800-CALL-NYS
www.iloveny.state.ny.us

North Carolina
800-VISIT-NC
919-733-4171
www.visitnc.com

North Dakota
800-HELLO-ND
www.ndtourism.com

Ohio
800-BUCKEYE
www.ohiotourism.com

Oklahoma
800-654-824
405-521-2409
www.touroklahoma.com

Oregon
800-547-7842
www.traveloregon.com

Pennsylvania
800-VISIT-PA
www.experiencepa.com

Rhode Island
800-556-2484
www.visitrhodeisland.com

South Carolina
800-346-3634
803-734-1700
www.travelsc.com

South Dakota
800-SDAKOTA
605-773-3301
www.travelsd.com

Tennessee
800-836-6200
615-741-2158
www.tourism.stat.tn.us/

Texas
800-452-9292
512-462-9191
www.state.tx.us/travel

Utah
800-200-1160
801-538-1030
www.state.ut.us/
visiting/travel.html

Vermont
800-VERMONT
802-828-3236
www.800-vermont.com

Virginia
800-932-5827
804-786-4484
www.virginia.org

Washington State
800-544-1800
360-586-2088
www.tourism.wa.gov

Washington DC
202-787-7000
www.washington.org

West Virginia
800-CALLWVA
304-558-2286
www.state.wv.us/tourism

Wisconsin
800-432-TRIP
608-266-2161
www.travelwisconsin.com

Wyoming
800-225-5996
307-777-7777
www.wyomingtourism.org

FOREIGN TOURIST OFFICES

ALGERIA
Embassy/Democratic & Popular
  Republic of Algeria
202-265-2800 / Fax: 202-667-2174

ARGENTINA
Argentina Government Tourism Office
213-930-0681 / Fax: 213-934-9076

AUSTRALIA
Australian Tourist Commission
310-552-1988 / Fax: 310-552-1215

AUSTRIA
Austrian National Tourist Office
212-944-6880 / Fax: 212-730-4568

BAHAMAS
Bahamas Tourist Offices
800-4-BAHAMA / 212-758-2777
  Fax: 212-753-6531

BELGIUM
Belgian National Tourist Office
212-758-8130 / Fax: 212-355-7675

BELIZE
Belize Tourist Board
800-624-0686 / 212-563-6011
  Fax: 212-563-6033

BOLIVIA
Embassy of The Republic of Bolivia
202-483-4410 / Fax: 202-328-3712

BRAZIL
Brazilian Consulate General
212-757-3080 / Fax: 212-956-3794

BRITISH VIRGIN ISLANDS
British Virgin Islands Tourist Board
800-835-8530 / 212-696-0400 /
  Fax: 212-949-8254

BULGARIA
Bulgaria Tourist Office
800-852-0944 / 212-573-5530 /
  Fax: 212-573-5538

CANADA
Canadian Embassy
202-682-1740 / Fax: 202-682-7721

CENTRAL AFRICAN REPUBLIC
Embassy/Central African Republic
202-483-7800 / Fax: 202-332-9893

CHILE
Embassy of the Republic of Chile
202-785-1746

CHINA
China National Tourist Office
212-760-9700 / Fax: 212-760-8809

COLOMBIA
Embassy of Colombia
202-387-8338 / Fax: 202-232-8643

CONGO
Permanent Mission of the People's
  Republic of the Congo
212-7447840 / Fax: 212-744-7875

COSTA RICA
Embassy of Costa Rica
202-234-2945/Fax: 202-265-4795

CUBA
Cuban Interest Section
202-797-8518 / Fax: 202-797-8521

CYPRUS
Cyprus Tourist Organization
212-683-5280 / Fax: 212-683-5282

CZECH REPUBLIC
Embassy of the Czech Republic
202-363-6315 / Fax: 202-966-8540

DENMARK
Danish Tourist Board
212-949-2333

DOMINICAN REPUBLIC
Embassy of the Dominican Republic
202-332-6280 / Fax: 202-265-8057

ECUADOR
Embassy of Ecuador
202-234-7166 / Fax: 202-667-3482

EGYPT
Egyptian Tourist Authority
312-280-4666 / 312-280-4788

ESTONIA
Embassy of the Rep of Estonia
202-789-0320 / Fax: 202-789-0471

ETHIOPIA
Embassy of Ethiopia
202-234-2281 / Fax: 202-328-7950

FINLAND
Finnish Tourist Board
800-346-4636 / 212-370-5540
    Fax: 212-983-5260

FRANCE
French Government Tourist Office
212-315-0888 /Fax: 212-247-6468

GALAPAGOS ISLANDS
Embassy of Ecuador
202-234-7200 / Fax: 202-667-3482

GERMANY
German National Tourist Office
212-661-7200 / Fax: 212-661-7174

GHANA
Embassy of Ghana
202-686-4500 / Fax: 202-686-4527

GREAT BRITAIN
British Tourist Authority
800-GO2-BRIT / 212-986-2200
    Fax: 212-986-1188

GREECE
Greek National Tourist Organization
212-421-5777 / Fax: 212-826-6940

GRENADA
Grenada Tourist Information Office
212-687-9554

GUATEMALA
Guatemala Tourist Commission
800-742-4529 / 305-442-0651
    Fax: 305-442-1013

HONG KONG
Hong Kong Tourist Association
212-869-5008 / Fax: 212-730-2605

HUNGARY
Ibusz Tourist Office
201-592-8585 / 201-592-8736

INDIA
Government of India Tourist Office
212-586-4901 / Fax: 212-582-3274

ICELAND
Iceland Tourist Board
212-949-2333 / Fax: 212-983-5260

INDONESIA
Indonesian Tourism Promotion Office
213-387-2078 / 213-386-4876

IRAN
Permanent Mission of Iran
212-687-2020

IRAQ
Permanent Mission of Iraq
212-737-4433

IRELAND
Irish Tourist Board
800-223 6470 / 212-418-0800
  Fax: 212-371-9052

ISRAEL
Israel Government Tourist Office
212-560-0600 / Fax: 212-627-4368

ITALY
Italian Government Tourist Office
310-820-0098 / Fax: 310-820-6357

JAMAICA
Jamaica Tourist Board
800-327-9857 /212-856-9727
  Fax: 212-856-9730

JAPAN
Japan National Tourist Organization
212-757-5640 / Fax: 212-307-6754

JORDAN
Jordan Information Bureau
202-265-1606 / Fax: 202-667-0777

KENYA
Kenya Tourist Office
310-274-6635 / Fax: 310-859-7010

KOREA
Korea National Tourism Corporation
213-382-3435 / Fax: 213-480-0483

KUWAIT
Consulate of Kuwait
212-973-4300 / Fax: 212-661-7263

LUXEMBOURG
Luxembourg National Tourist Office
212-935-8888 / Fax: 212-935-5896

MADAGASCAR
Madagascar Tourist Office
800-854-1029 / 619-792-6999 /
619-481-7474

MALAYSIA
Malaysian Tourist Information Center
213-689-9702 / Fax: 213-689-1530

MALTA
Malta National Tourist Office
212-695-9520 / Fax: 212695-8229

MEXICO
Mexican Government Tourism Office
212-755-7261 / Fax: 212-753-2874

MONACO
Monaco Government Tourist Bureau
212-759-5227 / Fax: 212-754-9320

MONGOLIA
Permanent Mission of Mongolia
212-861-9460 / Fax: 212-861-9464

MOROCCO
Moroccan National Tourist Office
212-557-2520 / Fax: 212-949-8148

MYANMAR
Permanent Mission of Myanmar
212-535-1310 / Fax: 212-737-2421

NEPAL
Permanent Mission of Nepal
212-370-4188 / Fax: 212-953-2038

NETHERLANDS
Netherlands Tourist Board
800-598-8500 / 312-819-0300
  Fax: 312-819-1740

NEW ZEALAND
New Zealand Tourism Board
800-388-5494 / 310-395-7480
  Fax: 310-395-5453

NIGERIA
Permanent Mission of Nigeria
212-953-9130 / Fax: 212-697-1970

NORTHERN IRELAND
800-326-0036 / 212-922-0101
  Fax: 212-922-0099

NORWAY
Norwegian Tourist Board
800-346-3436 / 212-949-2333
  Fax: 212-983-5260

PAPUA NEW GUINEA
Tourist Information/Air Niugini
714-752-5440 / 714-752-2160

PERU
Embassy of Peru
202-833-9860 / Fax: 202-659-8124

PHILIPPINES
Philippine Department of Tourism
212-575-7915 / Fax: 212-302-6759

POLAND
Polish National Tourist Office
312-236-9013 / Fax: 312-236-1125

PORTUGAL
Portuguese National Tourist Office
212-354-4403 / Fax: 212-764-6137

PUERTO RICO
Puerto Rico Tourism Company
800-815-7391/ 305-445-9112
  Fax: 305-445-9450

ROMANIA
Romanian National Tourist Office
212-697-6971 / Fax: 212-697-6972

RUSSIA
Intourist Travel Information Office
212-302-8161

SAUDI ARABIA
Royal Consulate of Saudi Arabia
212-752-2740 / Fax: 212-751-7000

SENEGAL
Senegal Tourist Office
800-HI-DAKAR / 212-757-7115
  Fax: 212-737-7461

SERBIA & MONTENEGRO
Permanent Mission of the Federal
  Republic of Yugoslavia
212-879-8700 / Fax: 212-879-8705

SIERRA LEONE
Permanent Mission of Sierra Leone
212-688-1656 / Fax: 212-688-4924

SINGAPORE
Singapore Tourist Promotion Board
312-938-1888 / Fax: 312-938-0086

SLOVENIA
Slovenian Tourist Office
212-682-5896 / Fax: 212-661-2469

SOUTH AFRICA
South African Tourism Board
800-822-5368 / 212-730-2929
  Fax: 212-764-1980

SPAIN
Tourist Office of Spain
212-759-8822 / Fax: 212-980-1053

SRI LANKA
Permanent Mission of Sri Lanka
212-986-7040 / Fax: 212-986-1838

SWEDEN
Swedish Travel & Tourism Council
212-949-2333 / Fax: 212-983-5260

SWITZERLAND
Swiss National Tourist Office
212-757-5944 / Fax: 212-262-6116

SYRIA
Consulate of the Syrian Arab Republic
713-781-8860

TAHITI
Tahiti Tourism
310-414-8484 / Fax: 310-414-8090

TAIWAN
Taiwan Visitors Association
212-466-0691 / Fax: 212-432-6436

TAJIKISTAN
Permanent Mission of Tajikistan
212-472-7645

TANZANIA
Permanent Mission of Tanzania
212-972-9160 / Fax: 212-682-5232

THAILAND
Tourism Authority of Thailand
212-432-0433 / Fax: 212-912-0920

TONGA
Tonga Consulate General
415-781-0365 / Fax: 415-781-3964

UNISIA
Permanent Mission of Tunisia
212-751-7503

TURKEY
Turkish Information Office
212-687-2194 / Fax: 212-599-7568

U.S. VIRGIN ISLANDS
U.S. Virgin Islands Division of Tourism
212-332-2222 / Fax: 212-332-2223

UGANDA
Permanent Mission of Uganda
212-949-0110

UKRAINE
Consulate General of Ukraine
212-371-5690 / Fax: 212-371-5547

URUGUAY
Tourist Office of Uruguay
305-443-7431 / 202-331-4219

VENEZUELA
Embassy of Venezuela
202-342-2214 / Fax: 202-342-6820

VIETNAM
Permanent Mission of Vietnam
212-213-5796 / Fax: 212-686-8534

YEMEN
Permanent Mission of Yemen
212-355-1730

YUGOSLAVIA
Permanent Mission of the Federal
   Republic of Yugoslavia
212-879-8700 / Fax: 212-879-8705

ZAMBIA
Zambia National Tourist Board
800-852-5998 / 212-308-2155
   Fax: 212-758-1319

ZIMBABWE
Zimbabwe Tourist Office
800-421-2381 / Fax: 212-332-1093

INDEX

Page numbers in **bold** indicate photographs.